SHIN BUDDHISM

DOUBLEDAY

New York London Toronto Sydney Auckland

SHIN BUDDHISM

Bits of Rubble
Turn into
Gold

TAITETSU UNNO

PUBLISHED BY DOUBLEDAY
a division of Random House, Inc.
1540 Broadway, New York, New York 10036

DOUBLEDAY and the portrayal of an anchor with a dolphin are trademarks of
Doubleday, a division of Random House, Inc.

The calligraphy on the cover is *muryoju* (Immeasurable Life),
and the calligraphy that separates the four parts of this book
is the original text for the English translation that appears in the Epilogue:
"How joyous I am, my heart and mind being rooted in the Buddha-ground
of the universal Vow, and my thoughts and feelings flowing within the
ocean of dharma that is beyond comprehension."
Both are by the author's late father, Enryo Unno (1903–1984).

Book design by Dana Leigh Treglia

Library of Congress Cataloging-in-Publication Data
Unno, Taitetsu, 1929–
Shin Buddhism : bits of rubble turn into gold / Taitetsu Unno.
p. cm.
Includes bibliographical references.
1. Shin (Sect)—Doctrines. 2. Religious life—Shin (Sect) I. Title.

BQ8718.3 .U55 2002
294.3'926—dc21
2001047571

ISBN 978-0-385-50469-0

To

Poets who are not Poets

Teachers who are not Teachers

Buddhists who are not Buddhists

Contents

Acknowledgments   xi
Preface   xiii
Prologue   1

PART ONE

Transformation

1. Rubble into Gold   11
2. Great Practice and Deep Hearing   23

3. Progressive Stages of Deep Hearing   30

4. Beyond the Psychological   37

5. Religion and Spirituality   43

6. Primal Vow   48

7. The Absolute Present   55

8. Time at Its Ultimate Limit   63

9. Shinjin as True Entrusting   67

10. A Path Less Taken   73

PART TWO

Unfolding Awareness

11. A Wasted Life   85

12. Self-Delusion   89

13. Subliminal Self   94

14. Symbolism of Light   98

15. Compassion that Nurtures   107

16. Living the Buddha Dharma   114

17. Personal and Social   123

PART THREE

Life as Creative Act

18. Creativity in Shin Life   131

19. Space as Metaphor   137

20. The World-Honored One   143

21. The Ordinary as Extraordinary   147

22. Two Parables   150

23. Life as Naturalness: Jinen   154

24. Life Beyond Our Control   160
25. Good and Evil   165

PART FOUR

Expanding Horizons

26. Three Grapefruits   175
27. Forgiveness   179
28. Caregiver Bodhisattva   184
29. The Inconceivable as Conceivable   193
30. The Inconceivable as Lived   197
31. Nirvana   204
32. Gratitude   208
33. Shinran's Wife   213
34. Critical Classification of Doctrines   222

    Epilogue   227
    Endnotes   233
    Glossary   253
    For Further Study   261
    Index   265

Acknowledgments

The appearance of any form of life, whether animate or inanimate, including a book like this, is the product of countless seen and unseen forces, multiple causes and conditions, the convergence of tentative planning and chance occurrences, and the ripening of time and circumstance.

The thought-provoking ideas and keen insights over the years that have come my way from friends of diverse backgrounds, fields of interest, and personal experiences have contributed to the formation of this book. They include members of the Shin Buddhist Sanghas in Northampton, Boston, and New York City, as well as Dharma friends across the country who have provided stimulating ideas to consider, inspiring books to read, diverse poets to quote, and challenging views to ponder.

They are too numerous to mention, but I wish to thank the following *kalyanamitras*, good spiritual guides and teachers, for their contributions to this book: Dimitri Bakhroushin, Geoffrey and Rebecca Brown, Mary Adele Combe, Cathy Fitzgerald, Caroline Forsman, Ty-Ranne Grimstad, Jean Higgins, Clement Hirae, Tatsuo Muneto, Todd Masuda, David Makinster, James and Alice Nagahiro, T. K. Nakagaki, Don Nunes, Corky Robinson, Chris Stetson, Eugene Tademaru, Hojo Tone, Mark Unno, Abram Yoshida, and Carol Zaleski.

In addition, I have also gained much from stimulating conversations with Jeanette Arakawa, Jake Bassett, Isabelle Bernard, Alfred Bloom, Pat Deer, Mina Harrison, Kimi and Clarence Hisatsune, AnnaMarie Russo, Richard St. Clair, Ruth Tabrah, Alice Unno, Jeff Wilson, and Sets Yoshida. They all spent considerable time reading the original manuscript and making pertinent suggestions to improve both its contents and style. I want to thank them all.

Finally, I wish to acknowledge my great debt to Trace Murphy for his invaluable support and professional advice that has made possible this little book, as well as my earlier work, *River of Fire, River of Water*. In spite of his demanding schedule he consented to writing a preface that is both generous and insightful for which I express my deepest appreciation.

Taitetsu Unno
Northampton, MA
April 8, 2002

Preface

It has been a great privilege for me to help make this work available to the public in my capacity as an editor at Doubleday. I have no special knowledge of the subject, only knowledge of the task of making books. So it surprised and honored me that I was asked to contribute a few words at the start.

I was fortunate to have been introduced to the author through his son, Dr. Mark Unno, also a scholar of Buddhism, currently at the University of Oregon. A project of his had been brought to my attention by

Sienna Craig (then a colleague at Doubleday), and in time through him I became familiar with his father's work and esteemed reputation at Smith College and beyond.

When I first contacted Dr. Taitetsu Unno we discussed a book that might introduce general readers to the aspect of compassion in *Jodo Shinshu,* which seemed to me not well understood on a popular level. There were significant resources available in the West for Zen and Tibetan Buddhism (and increasingly for Vipassana) but references to Pure Land were often dismissive and sometimes negative.

The result of those conversations was his *River of Fire, River of Water,* a series of reflections on various elements of Shin Buddhism that creatively balanced scholarship, verses, allegories, and personal anecdotes. This book was well received and as of this writing has almost sold through its fifth printing. Based on the feedback that we received, there seemed to be more that people wanted to know about Shin, and fortunately there is much more that he has to share. Where *River of Fire, River of Water* offered an assortment, *Shin Buddhism* gives a more complete overview of the tradition.

While it is too early to say how these books will fit into the future library of Buddhism in America, I have a strong feeling that they add an important dimension. Perhaps it is too grandiose a statement (I certainly am far from being an unbiased observer), but for me they feel appropriately placed alongside the more influential books of the past few decades. Besides presenting another of the "eighty-four thousand paths to liberation," they enrich our resources by making plain the necessary link between daily life and spiritual life, between the mundane and the transcendent.

This, of course, is exclusive neither to Dr. Unno's work nor to Shin Buddhism—indeed it seems an obvious insight. Not a week goes by when I am not introduced to at least a few projects (published or unpublished) whose goal is to integrate some form of spiritual practice with ordinary living. But what he shows is not just an integration of differing though somewhat compatible elements. He shows the continuity between, and the shared nature of the bits of rubble and the gold. When we hear about his frustrating experience in amateur marriage counseling or his dream involving Hills Brothers coffee, we may not immediately be reminded of Joshu's dog or Kasyapa smiling at the flower. But they are examples with which we can probably identify immediately, and they encourage us at a time when we may feel that there is a permanent wall between ourselves and enlightenment. In other words, perhaps Dr. Unno's biggest contribution has been to guide us back to the rediscovery of our own, nonexotic selves.

When I think back on my initial conversations about compassion with Dr. Unno, I am impressed by how much I have since learned on the subject from working with him. Not only have I learned of "the Name-that-calls," the boundless compassion that sustains all life, but I have seen the compassion working through him. His great intelligence, personal warmth, and his generosity of self (on the page and off) have been a rich source of wisdom to contemplate. As he has for many others, he has been a great teacher for me. I am glad that through this book he continues to make himself and his knowledge available to many thousands out in the world.

Trace Murphy
Executive Editor, Doubleday

SHIN BUDDHISM

Prologue

Buddhism is a living organism, like a mighty oak tree that has deep roots in the earth and extends its branches toward the sky. The roots grow downward into the earth, anchoring the tree and absorbing nutrients, while the branches and leaves, nurtured by the sun, provide shelter from the blazing heat, protection from wind and rain, and a resting place for weary travelers.

In the history of humankind the seeds of this mighty tree were planted in India in the fifth century

1

B.C.E., and its rudimentary roots spread into the soils of various countries of the Asian continent. Today, they are spreading to the world over, especially into the North American soil, seeking new sources of moisture and nutrients. The main branches that appeared were Theravada Buddhism in Southeast Asia and Mahayana Buddhism in Central and East Asia, giving rise to diverse branches and offshoots.

The spreading branches and countless leaves evident to our eyes may be likened to the various teachings, practices, and schools of Buddhism that have flourished, while the soil and earth constitute their root source, embracing all animate and inanimate existence. The latter cannot really thrive by itself alone; it needs the branches and leaves to survive. And the former, too, will remain nothing but human constructs, unless constantly nourished by the source of life itself.

Among the many branches of this mighty tree, the better-known ones in North America are today represented by various forms of Zen, Tibetan Buddhism, and Vipassana practices, but there are many other branches that are found in the Asian landscape. One of them is the Pure Land branch of Mahayana Buddhism, whose deep roots go back to the South Asian world that produced many scriptures, including the Pure Land scriptures, in the first century B.C.E. A major offshoot of this branch that emerged in thirteenth-century Japan is Jodo-Shinshu or Shin Buddhism.

While Theravada Buddhism venerates a single Buddha, the historical Shakyamuni, Mahayana Buddhism has many Buddhas that play principal roles in the different scriptures. They include such names as Akshobhya Buddha, Maitreya Buddha, Vairochana Buddha, Bhaishajyaguru Buddha, and Amitabha or Amitayus Buddha, who is the Buddha in the Pure Land scriptures. In East Asian Buddhism the two titles—Amitabha, Immeasurable Light, and Amitayus, Immeasurable Life—are combined into the contracted form Amita or Amida.

The two primary scriptures of Pure Land that originated in India are called the *Larger Sukhavati-vyuha Sutra* and the *Smaller Sukhavati-vyuha Sutra*. *Sukhavati-vyuha* means the "adornment of the realm of bliss." They will be referred to simply as the Larger Sutra and the Smaller Sutra in our text. A third scripture of Central Asian or Chinese origin, dating from about the fourth century C.E., is the *Kuan wu-liang-shou ching* or the *Sutra on the Contemplation of the Buddha of Immeasurable Life* (abbreviated to Contemplation Sutra). These three are called the Triple Sutras of Pure Land Buddhism.[1]

The Larger Sutra describes the career of a bodhisattva, a potential Buddha-to-be, by the name of Dharmakara, who makes forty-eight vows before another Buddha, known as Sovereign Monarch of the World. The vows promise to relieve the sufferings of people and replace them with peace and comfort. When Dharmakara fulfills and completes all the vows, he attains Buddhahood and becomes known as Amida Buddha. The most important among them is the Eighteenth Vow, also called the Primal Vow, which manifests the nonjudgmental and all-embracing compassion of Amida. Dharmakara's spiritual evolution is said to be patterned after the life of the historical Buddha in a mytho-poetic form, so that it might have universal appeal.

The Smaller Sutra is a highly imaginative portrayal of the realm of enlightenment in very concrete terms: bejeweled railings, nettings, trees; bathing pools lined with golden sands with steps of gold, silver, lapis lazuli, and crystal; pavilions covered with exquisite jewels built on the earth made of gold. The atmosphere is filled with celestial music, rare and exquisite birds, and a subtle breeze blowing through jeweled trees which produces a melodious chorus. This rich and colorful description is said to be a manifestation of emptiness *(shunyata)* that expresses itself freely in any way it chooses. Since reality is empty of permanent being and all things are in flux, it can take any form.

The Contemplation Sutra begins with the tragedy of

3

Rajagriha, which occurred during the time of the historical Buddha. Prince Ajatasatru, incited by Devadatta, a cousin and rival of Shakyamuni, imprisons his father the king and later his mother the queen. In distress, the Queen, Vaidehi, calls for Shakyamuni Buddha to counsel her. The Buddha shows countless Pure Lands, among which Vaidehi selects the Pure Land of Amida and aspires to be born in that land. The Buddha describes sixteen forms of contemplation by which birth in the Pure Land is assured.

The Pure Land scriptures were popularized in China, and various lineages of practice derived from them evolved. Important commentaries and studies began appearing beginning in the fourth century C.E. When these scriptures were introduced into Japan in the sixth century, they did not attract much attention, but gradually they inspired monks and nuns among the six schools of the Nara Period (710–794) to pursue Pure Land practices. It was in the Heian Period (794–1191), however, that Pure Land beliefs began to have a major impact on some of the monastic institutions and the general culture. It became an inspiration for art and architecture, as well as for poetry and literature, producing, for example, the first major narrative in world literature, *The Tale of Genji* by Lady Murasaki, in the eleventh century. The two Buddhist schools of Heian, known as Shingon and Tendai, also embraced aspects of Pure Land teachings, but it is the Tendai practice known as the Samadhi of Constant Practice that is significant for our purposes. This practice, originally conceived by Chih-I (538–597), the founder of the T'ien-t'ai school in China, was a ninety-day circumambulation of the image of Amida Buddha, constantly reciting the name of Amida with almost no rest or sleep.

A charismatic figure by the name of Honen, a monk of the Tendai order, appeared and proclaimed the founding of a separate and independent Pure Land school, called Jodo-shu, in 1175 C.E. (*Jodo* means "Pure Land" and *shu* is "school.") His basic tenet is summed up in the phrase, "In the path of Sages one perfects wisdom and achieves enlightenment; in the path of Pure Land one returns to the foolish self to be saved by Amida." The basic practice that Honen recommended was the single-hearted recitation of *nembutsu,* the Name of Amida: NAMU-AMIDA-BUTSU.

Among Honen's many followers, it was Shinran (1173–1263) who followed in his footsteps to penetrate the inner dynamics of intoning the nembutsu, rejecting mechanical repetition and clarifying its source as the boundless compassion that is Amida Buddha. Thus, the saying of nembutsu is experienced as a call from Amida, but simultaneously it is our response to that call. Being a devoted student of Honen, Shinran disclaimed any following, but his lineage kept alive his memory and teaching, which eventually became recognized as another Pure Land school, known as Jodo-shinshu. Although Shinran used the term Jodo-shinshu to mean "the true and real tenet of Pure Land (as taught by Honen)," today it is used as the name of an independent school, widely referred to in the West as Shin Buddhism.

The question most frequently asked of a Shin Buddhist is, What is your practice? As a Buddhist, the obvious answer is the practice of compassion. Our task is to manifest compassion in everyday life, beginning with members of our own families and extending it to all of society. But when one really tries to practice compassion, expressing care, concern, empathy, and love, all the while respecting the autonomy and dignity of the other, one encounters a huge obstacle. And that obstacle is never the other, but one's own self-centered ego. This awareness is the starting point of the Shin Buddhist path.

When we are made aware of this neglected aspect of ourselves, hidden in darkness, which hinders our practice of compassion on a consistent, thoroughgoing basis, we are already being touched by the light of boundless compassion that is Amida Buddha. This light not only illuminates our darkness, it transforms it, so that we try to be compassionate with a sense of humility and gratitude, mindful of our karmic limitations. Humility arises for having been shown our karma-bound self, yet we are grateful for the boundless compassion that inspires us to act with a new and vigorous appreciation for life. All this is contained in the saying of *nembutsu:* NAMU-AMIDA-BUTSU. It consists of two parts integrated as one: the being of self-enclosure and deep egocentricity, symbolized by *namu,* illuminated and transformed by boundless compassion, *amida-butsu.* In sum, living the nembutsu becomes the ultimate practice of a Shin Buddhist.

樹心弘誓佛地

流念舊恩法海

釋華書

樹心弘誓佛地

流念難思法海

釋華書

PART ONE

Transformation

1

Rubble into Gold

Buddhism is a path of supreme optimism, for one of
its basic tenets is that no human life or experience is
to be wasted, abandoned, or forgotten, but all should
be transformed into a source of vibrant life, deep wisdom, and compassionate living. This is the connotation of the classical statement that sums up the goal of
Buddhist life: "Transform delusion into enlightenment." On the everyday level of experience, Shin
Buddhists speak of this transformation as "bits of rubble turn into gold."

This metaphor comes from Tz'u-min, the Chinese Pure Land master of the eighth century, who proclaims the working of boundless compassion of Amida, the Buddha of Immeasurable Light and Life, as follows:

> *The Buddha, in the causal stage, made the*
> *universal vow:*
> *When beings hear my Name and think on me,*
> *I will come to welcome each of them,*
> *Not discriminating at all between the poor*
> *and the rich and well-born,*
> *Not discriminating between the inferior and*
> *highly gifted,*
> *Not choosing the learned and those upholding*
> *pure precepts,*
> *Nor rejecting those who break precepts and*
> *whose evil karma is profound.*
> *Solely making beings turn about and*
> *abundantly say the nembutsu,*
> *I can make bits of rubble change into gold.*[1]

This transformation expresses the boundless compassion, non-judgmental and all-inclusive, that is the moving force in the Buddhist tradition. It is not, however, a simple, naive optimism, for the starting point of Buddhism is a recognition of the universal fact of human suffering, born of both personal and collective karma. In fact, it is a realistic appraisal of life as it is, not merely on the surface of things but at its most profound depth. In this depth, abundant with the accumulated pain and sorrow of humanity, is also found the capacity of the human spirit to achieve its fullest potential, no matter the obstacles, through awakening to the working of boundless compassion deep within our life.

This awakening is brought about through the nembutsu, NAMU-AMIDA-BUTSU, the calling from Amida Buddha, and we acknowledge it in our saying of the nembutsu. The radical transformation involved in this simple act will be explored from various angles, but let us turn to some concrete examples of what we mean by the transformative experience central to the Buddhist tradition.

A framed photograph of a broomstick on my office wall, taken by Maria, one of my former students, reminds me of the great compassion of Shakyamuni Buddha which brought about the transformation of the lowly monk Culapanthaka to become one of the most respected figures in early Buddhism.[2] His older brother, Mahapanthaka, was celebrated as an articulate and wise monk, a commanding figure in the Sangha, while Culapanthaka was the very opposite: dim-witted and bumbling in speech. Unable to memorize even a single line of the teaching, he was the object of ridicule by his fellow monks. He regarded himself as a total failure; his inferiority complex knew no end.

One day when the Buddha saw Culapanthaka in tears, having been ordered by his brother to return to lay status, he called him aside and assured him of help on the path of enlightenment. The Buddha showed empathy for his plight and gave him a simple refrain to repeat each time he swept the monastic compound as part of his daily task: "Take away the dirt, sweep away the dust." After rehearsing and repeating this phrase countless times, even though he sometimes forgot the precise wording, Culapanthaka attained a breakthrough. The constant repetition affected the deepest layer of his psyche, as he realized that dirt and dust are defilements (*klesha*) to be taken away and swept away by wisdom (*prajna*). It was the Buddha's felt pain that touched Culapanthaka's pain and elicited this transformation.

The Buddha's compassion is the basis for the parable of the four horses that he preached when he resided at the Kalandaka Grove.[3] The first horse, he explained, runs swiftly the instant he sees the shadow of a whip. The next horse will run fast the moment his skin feels the whip. The third horse runs when the whip cuts into his flesh. The slowest horse will run only after repeated lashings. Quoting this parable of the four horses, Shunryu Suzuki states in *Zen Mind, Beginner's Mind*:

> If you think the aim of Zen practice is to train you to be-
> come one of the best horses, you will have a big problem.
> This is not the right understanding. . . . If you consider the
> mercy of the Buddha, how do you think Buddha will feel
> about the four kinds of horses? He will have more sympathy
> for the worst one than for the best one.[4]

This highly respected teacher, Suzuki Roshi, identifies with the slowest horse; his Zen practice is sustained and developed by virtue of the compassion of the Buddha.

Although Suzuki does not mention it, the scripture actually uses the parable of the four horses in order to describe four kinds of people on the path of Buddhism. The first kind awakens and moves forward on the path the instant they *hear* about the suffer-ings caused by old age, illness, and death, acknowledging the Four Noble Truths taught by Shakyamuni Buddha: suffering, its cause, its cessation, and the means to that cessation. The second kind moves when they not only hear but actually *see* with their own eyes the sufferings of people caused by old age, illness, and death. The third kind is not affected at all by the sufferings of others, but when a family member experiences sufferings due to old age, ill-ness, and death, they move forward on the path. And the fourth kind is not distressed at all by seeing old age, illness, and death in others or even among family members, but they are jolted and pushed forward on the path when they personally experience the sufferings that accompany old age, illness, and death.

Just as the sympathy of the Buddha identifies with the slowest horse, the compassion of the Buddha focuses on this last group of people, which includes most of us. But some of us do not easily awaken to the meaning of life's evanescence, filled with unexpected tragedies and culminating in death, even if we personally experience them. When we finally do feel a need, it may be too late, because old age limits our physical and mental capacities, illness prohibits any sustained quest, and death obliterates everything. Such people are called foolish beings (*bonbu*).

Foolish beings, however, are the primary concern of Amida, and it is upon them that the flooding light of boundless compassion shines, eventually bringing about a radical transformation in life—hopeless to hopeful, darkness to light, ignorance to enlightenment, bits of rubble to gold. This awareness of foolish beings is at the core of Japanese Buddhist life, regardless of school or denomination. The term *bonbu* appears as early as the seventh century C.E. in the Seventeen Articles by Prince Shotoku, the father of Japanese Buddhism, who formulated this guideline for an ideal government.[5] What does it mean to say that the focus of boundless compassion is the foolish being?

At a Shin temple in Japan, I once heard a teacher talk about his only son, who had had a terrible case of asthma since the time he was born. Hoping for a cure before the boy entered first grade so he could receive normal schooling, they moved south with him to a warmer climate. The boy slowly grew stronger, strong enough to enter primary school with his peers. One of the first major events in the Japanese school year is what is called Field Day, when all students participate in some kind of race according to their grade level.

Early in the morning of Field Day, the little boy went to school accompanied by his mother. As the father waited for their return home later that day, he could hear gleeful laughter and happy conversation coming from the two as they approached their home. Sensing their excitement, the father thought for sure that his son must have done well in his race. As soon as the two entered the house, he called out to his son, asking, "Did you take first place in

your race?" "No, Dad," the boy shouted, "I didn't come in first—
I came in eighth!" "Oh," the father said, "And how many kids ran
in your race?" "Eight!" the son shouted, clapping his hands.

The mother turned to the father with a big smile. "Isn't it
wonderful that he could run just like the other children? He came
in eighth place; he finished the race! Remember when he couldn't
even run at all? Now he runs just like the other children. This is
cause for celebration! Our son is Number One!" With this story,
the teacher reminded us that within boundless compassion each of
us is Number One, whether in last place or not. In fact, it is the
last-place finisher, the foolish being, who is first in the eyes of
Amida Buddha.

The realization that one is a foolish being occurs constantly
and can be demonstrated by mundane examples taken from everyday life. It happened to me once when I came across an evaluation
of my teaching. At the college where I taught for almost thirty
years, there are two surveys that evaluate courses and professors.
An official survey is conducted by the dean of faculty, and the report is sent to every faculty member. There is, however, an underground survey compiled by students, called "Aspects," that is
not shown to the faculty.

But one day I happened to come across a copy of "Aspects"
that listed two of my courses. The introductory course on world
religions was team-taught and had the following brief comment:
"The course was team-taught. Miss Higgins and Mr. Hubbard
were clear and to the point, but Mr. Unno was vague and never
gave straight answers."

This criticism was painful, because I had always considered
myself a good teacher and lecturer. This was harsh. But my deflated ego was immediately soothed when I read the next remark
by another student, "Mr. Unno is wonderful. He is really clear and
cares."

Before my inflated ego could congratulate itself, I was shattered by another critique of my course on Buddhist Thought. I

took great pride in this course, and I had inspired many students to explore the subject further. The negative comment read: "Discussion was *not* encouraged and the professor was *not* interested in hearing others' viewpoints."

Again, my ego was deflated with a hissing sound that was almost audible. But the next sentence saved my day: "Professor Unno is excellent. He generates enthusiasm, and his anecdotes all pertain to the subject matter."

A few words randomly tossed out by students, probably long forgotten by them, can easily create upheavals in a professor's self-image. Whenever we feel anxiety and experience insecurity, or we become bubbly with success and excitement, we are surely showing signs of a foolish being drowning in *samsara,* the ocean of birth and death. But it is such a foolish being, awakened by the working of boundless compassion, who undergoes transformation to eventually become a true, real, and sincere human being.

We see a vivid example of nembutsu awakening in the life of Hisako Nakamura (1897–1961), who lost both her hands and feet at the age of three, due to a gangrene infection caused by frostbite.[6] She grew up in poverty and suffered discrimination because of her condition. Her only means of livelihood was to be featured in a sideshow exhibition, performing everything a normal person could do—cooking, eating, sewing, writing, bathing, cleaning, and so on. She thus traveled throughout Japan, Taiwan, Korea, and Manchuria for twenty-two years. Helen Keller, whom she met for the first time in 1937, is said to have admired Nakamura for her strength and courage.[7]

Over the years she was married four times—losing two husbands by death and one by divorce—and had two daughters. When she encountered the Shin teachings in her sixties, she found a path that affirmed her life as it was. It helped her reject the advice of friends who told her to accept her situation. Instead, Nakamura found herself existing within boundless compassion that not only shouldered the burdens of her life as its ultimate concern but provided the energy and strength for her to live each day positively and vigorously. In her words,

> *After a moment of irritability, I reflect.*
> *And prostrate myself before the Buddha.*
> *What should I do about my selfish desires?*
> *I can only leave it in the hands of the Buddha.*

> *The white chrysanthemums I offer the Buddha*
> *Its pure odor remains as I chant the morning* sutra.
> *The cheapest of rice gruel (that I am)*
> *That allows me to live.*

> *The worship that brings such happiness,*
> *The* karma *that the mother bears,*
> *And the* karma *that she forces her daughters to bear*
> *Are all borne by the Buddha*
> *(So I must do my part by living to the fullest today).*

> *Sixty years without hands or feet*
> *Only because the Buddha's*
> *Compassionate hands and feet*
> *Have taken the place of mine.*[8]

Later in life Nakamura was in constant demand as a speaker, not only at Buddhist gatherings but at schools, prisons, disabled veterans associations, and mothers' groups, sharing her experiences and her faith to overcome insurmountable difficulties. She traveled all over the country, carried on the backs of her husband and daughters, to inspire people to live positively and gratefully, cherishing this unrepeatable human life.

Transformation occurs not only in life but in death. We find this in the life story of another devout Shin Buddhist, Kichibei (1803–1881), who fell in love with a woman as a young man and had a child out of wedlock.⁹ Although he sought to marry her, his wish was denied by both families, for each was a single child, expected to carry on their respective family names, according to a time-honored Japanese custom. Broken-hearted, angry, and upset, Kichibei became acutely aware of the contradiction that he deeply felt—the yearning of the heart denied by social conventions.

Kichibei turned to the Buddha Dharma, seeking solace and some kind of resolution. When he pursued it, rather than finding an answer, he was confronted with a monumental contradiction: death abruptly negates everything in life. This spurred him on to immerse himself even more deeply in his quest for meaning. Although it took him almost a lifetime of grappling with the question of death and dying, he reached a deep appreciation for the preciousness of this fragile life on earth, prompted by an awareness that death can instantly end this human life, a life that can never be repeated in eternity. Buddhism does not negate life but affirms life, including everything within it—despair, frustration, and anger in the case of youthful Kichibei. Everything negative is now seen in a radically different light and is transformed into a positive experience.

My friend Lily lost her husband a year ago. Through her tragic loss, with its grief, pain, sorrow, and loneliness, she awakened to the preciousness of life here and now. It was the crowning result of many years of deep hearing, a crucial pursuit on the Shin path. Deep hearing means continual engagement with the teaching, Buddha Dharma—questioning, doubting, reflecting, forgetting, remembering. Regardless of how much one may or may not absorb the words of the Buddha on the conscious level, something more important is taking place in the subconscious—what I call *sedimentation*.

Sedimentation involves continual absorption of the teaching, deep hearing of the call of Amida, its saturation into one's total being, and its sudden, unexpected appearance, like a long-forgotten childhood memory, to help us through times of need and distress. It may surface, for example, when we experience the loss of a loved one, to help us not only to endure the pain but to appreciate the loss. This happened to Lily in her experience of losing her husband. In her simple, straightforward manner she recounts:

> *His debilitating illness*
> *And eventual death awakened in me*
> *The great boundless compassion*
> *And wisdom of Amida.*
> *Ah! How grateful I am*
> *For the peace and joy that I discovered*
> *In the here and now.*[10]

In the awakening to the preciousness of the here and now, Lily is reborn and so is her husband, who now comes fully alive as a continuing presence in her life. Morrie Schwartz states in *Tuesdays with Morrie,* "death ends a life but not a relationship."[11] A new and enduring relationship has now been established between Lily and her husband.

Simply put, transformation here includes the realization that affirming death simultaneously affirms life. Although couched in different languages, depending on the culture and context, a similar point is made throughout the world, especially by sensitive poets, thinkers, and artists, formulated in their unique ways. The German poet Rainer Maria Rilke, for example, states in his correspondence with Countess Margot Sizzo, dated January 6, 1923:

> I will not say that one should *love* death; but one should love life so magnanimously, so without calculation and selection that spontaneously one constantly includes with it and loves death too (life's averted half),—which is in fact what happens also, irresistibly and illimitably, in all great impulses of

love! Only because we exclude death in a sudden moment of reflection, has it turned more and more into something alien, and as we have kept it in the alien, something hostile.[12]

This is the central theme in Rilke's celebrated *Duino Elegies,* as he explains to his Polish translator: *"Death is the side of life* averted from us, unshone upon by us: we must try to achieve the greatest consciousness of our existence which is at home in *both unbounded realms, inexhaustibly nourished from both."*[13]

Within the working of boundless compassion, anything can thus be transformed to become life-affirming and life-enhancing. This is not the result of human ingenuity, calculation, or design, nor is it based on some vague hope or anticipation. It comes about through the working of boundless compassion, beyond our conceptual understanding, entering our hearts and minds to effect a radical change in our views of self and the world.

The paramount transformation in Mahayana Buddhism occurs when even a foolish being attains Buddhahood by the wondrous working of boundless compassion. According to Shinran, the founder of Shin Buddhism:

Needless to say, our Buddha Amida grasps beings with the Name. Thus, as we hear it with our ears and say it with our lips, exalted virtues without limit grasp and pervade our hearts and minds. It becomes ever after the seed of our Buddhahood, all at once sweeping away a *koti* of kalpas of heavy karmic evil, and we attain the realization of supreme enlightenment. I know truly that the Name possesses not scant roots of good but inexhaustible roots of good.[14]

The Name, NAMU-AMIDA-BUTSU, contains inexhaustible roots of good, for its power of transformation knows no bounds, transforming those with "heavy karmic evil" into beings of supreme enlightenment. A foolish being does not choose to be foolish; it is the consequence of deep past karma ("koti of kalpas" means in-conceivable eons of time), and yet one must take full responsibility for oneself. Since our foolishness creates unhappiness for both ourselves and others, it is considered evil. Yet boundless compassion focuses on such a foolish being of heavy karmic evil to eventually bring about the attainment of supreme enlightenment.

Though we may be unaware, the Shin Buddhist path reminds us that the marvel of transformation abounds in the world wherever the human spirit endures and soars. Bits of rubble turn into gold everywhere, if only we have eyes to see and heart to embrace the impossible possibility.

2

Great Practice and Deep Hearing

In Shin Buddhism the ultimate goal of transformation occurs in the saying of nembutsu, NAMU-AMIDA-BUTSU. What does this mean? In brief, the nembutsu is the flowing call of the Buddha of Immeasurable Light and Life, coming from the fathomless center of life itself, as well as our response to that call without any hesitation or calculation. Thus, it is not a petitionary act, a mindless, mechanical repetition, or a mantra with magical powers. This requires some explanation.

This calling of nembutsu awakens us to a liberating power that sanctifies all life, because it comes from beyond the small-minded self that is always engaged in calculating life only in terms of gain or loss, winning or losing. Sooner or later we will respond to this call, if we are ever to know a sense of security and well-being. If I were to translate nembutsu into English, it would be the "Name-that-calls," for it calls us to awaken to our fullest potential to becoming true, real, and sincere human beings.

What is essential, then, is not the number of times voiced, nor even the purity of heart involved, but simply the deep hearing of the Name-that-calls to which we want to respond. Shinran formulates this in the language of the Pure Land tradition:

> The great practice is to say the Name of the Tathagata of un-hindered light. This practice, embodying all good acts and possessing all roots of virtue, is perfect and most rapid in bringing them to fullness. It is the treasure ocean of virtues that is suchness or true reality. For this reason it is called great practice. This practice arises from the Vow of great compassion.[1]

The expression "great practice" has transcendental significance, because the adjective "great" refers to the Buddha, and "practice" connotes the salvific activity of the Buddha actualized in foolish beings. Great practice is the product of the Primal Vow that has already been fulfilled by boundless compassion to save all beings. Hence, the sounding of the Name is the life of Amida Buddha coursing through our bodies. Shinran identifies its source when he concludes that "This practice arises from the Vow of great compassion." When we are made to realize that the Vow of liberation and freedom is directed to each of us, we cannot but respond by intoning the Name, NAMU-AMIDA-BUTSU.

The "Tathagata of unhindered light" is another name for Amida Buddha. Tathagata, a synonym for Buddha, is the "one who comes to us from the world of Reality-as-it-is" and whose sole purpose is the illumination of our darkness and its transformation. Nothing can hinder or obstruct its working, hence the title "unhindered light." Since it is the Buddha's salvific activity being actualized in a person, each utterance of the Name brings to fullness "all good acts" and "all roots of virtue." In general Buddhism we would call this realizing suchness (*tathata*), metaphorically referred to here as the "treasure ocean of virtues." In sum, this practice, then, is not my practice but *great* practice, the working of boundless compassion becoming manifest in each saying of the Name. "Saying" in the Japanese original is *mosu*, a term that is not simply verbal but somatic, involving one's whole being, a voicing coming from both the conscious and unconscious depths.

This practice of recitative nembutsu changed the course of Japanese Buddhism, for the monastic paths, patronized by the imperial court and the nobility, had excluded the masses until 1175 C.E., when Honen founded an independent Jodo school. Then the gates to liberation and freedom were wide open, welcoming those who had hitherto been excluded: women of all classes; hunters, butchers, and fishermen, who took life to make a living; peasants and merchants considered ignorant and "bad" in the eyes of the upper classes; and monks and nuns who had violated the precepts.

Now, one embodies great practice, the working of boundless compassion in one's life, through deep hearing, to ultimately realize that one is "grasped, never to be abandoned" (*sesshu-fusha*). In the words of Shinran,

> Wholly sincere, indeed, are the words of truth that one is grasped, never to be abandoned, the right dharma all-surpassing and wondrous! Hear and reflect, and let there be no wavering or apprehension.[2]

This engagement transcends ordinary dualistic experience, in which we separate the subject and the object. In contrast, "grasped, never to be abandoned" suggests a nondual mode of apprehension. We might liken this to hearing music in the true sense, as exemplified by the famous lines from *The Dry Salvages* by T. S. Eliot:

> *Music heard so deeply*
> *that is not heard at all.*
> *And you are the music,*
> *while the music lasts.*[3]

When listening to music, objectively speaking, there is of course the one who listens and the music that is heard, but such a distinction is purely conceptual and nonexistent in the deep hearing of music. Deep hearing is nondualistic, in contrast to the dualistic, which objectifies everything, even one's own emotions. The nembutsu is the music of cosmic harmony, which reverberates through one's being in the sounding of NAMU-AMIDA-BUTSU.

Such is the experience of deep hearing, which is more than merely intellectual or cognitive; it involves a complete transformation involving bodily behavior. What this means can be illustrated by taking the example of cigarette smoking. Anyone can understand the warning label on a pack of cigarettes: "SURGEON GENERAL'S WARNING: Smoking causes lung cancer, heart disease, emphysema, and may complicate pregnancy." If a lifelong nicotine addict reads this and stops smoking, he has embodied the message completely. It has been fully internalized, changing his lifestyle. However, if the addict does not stop smoking, his understanding is purely cerebral. From a Buddhist standpoint, it is a superficial hearing that does not effect any behavioral change.

In Buddhist literature we often come across the word "realize." This word has two connotations. First, it means to see or understand clearly, such as in the admission "I realized my mistake." Second, it is to make something real, total, and concrete, as in the saying "He realized his dream." The dream has been completely embodied. It is in the latter sense that we speak of realizing enlightenment or realizing Buddhahood. The purpose of Buddhist practice is to go beyond the first sense of understanding something to the second sense of embodiment. In this sense, saying the nembutsu, realizing the reason for it, is the same as living the nembutsu.

The goal of deep hearing, then, is to bring about a fundamental change in one's life, such that one realizes liberation and freedom in the midst of worldly entanglements, daily responsibilities, and constant agitations. This path is for everyone, especially lay people, in our contemporary world, because the nembutsu path has no requirements except the recognition of an indisputable fact: *The problems in our daily life can be ultimately transmuted into sources of self-knowledge and received wisdom.* With this conviction, we engage in deep hearing that eventually culminates in a settled and secure state. Or, to put it differently, "Through hearing (embodying) that the Buddha's majestic virtue is great and vast, one attains the stage of non-retrogression."[4]

The process of deep hearing, broadly speaking, consists of five stages that are interrelated. First is receptivity to the teaching. If you want a bowl of soup, you must come with an empty bowl ready to receive the soup. Second is unfolding awareness of its message in one's own life. One must not simply carry around the bowlful of soup; one must drink it, empty its contents, and make it a source of nourishment and energy. Third is the interplay of light and darkness. The nourishment received heightens our sensitivity to movements in the world, both internal and external, revealing the subtle egocentric stirrings within us, illuminated by the light of compassion. That is, in everything we think, say, and do, we are shown the reciprocity of blind passion and boundless compassion, darkness of ignorance and light of true reality. Fourth is

27

deep hearing of the nembutsu, the call from the heart of bound-less compassion that spontaneously transforms darkness into light and ignorance into wisdom. The light of compassion is warm and nurturing, not cold, harsh, or glaring. It transforms the negative into positive. And fifth is the subsequent life of gratitude, whereby everyday life becomes the training ground, or *dojo,* for karma-bound beings of foolishness to meet the challenges of the world creatively and effectively.

The distinction into the five stages is arbitrary, a tentative out-line to help the seeker on a journey of becoming and self-discovery. Actually, the five overlap and interpenetrate in a dynamic process that cannot be circumscribed or terminated at any point. In fact, in the final stage, where one is confronted with difficult issues in daily living, the creative response comes from continued receptivity to the teaching, which quickens the awareness of the constant inter-play of light and darkness and subsequent transformation, all expe-rienced with a renewed sense of gratitude at every turn.

As long as we remain limited, finite karmic beings, we can never transcend *samsara,* the ocean of birth-and-death, but once we awaken to the working of boundless compassion, we no longer create further karmic acts that chain us to repeated delusions. From this is born my personal aspiration, as I once reminded myself:

Awakening is dynamic,
Constantly evolving with life's realities—
Unfolding from ego self to compassionate self,
From enclosed self to open self,
From foolish self to enlightened self.[5]

The ultimate realization for limited, karmic beings awaits to be fully and completely realized in the Pure Land.

The process of deep hearing culminates with our birth in Pure Land, but the Pure Land is not the ultimate goal. It is a mere way station from which we return into our world of samsara. Now endowed with wisdom and compassion, the welfare and salvation of all beings become the ultimate concern. The return, however, is inseparable from the going, both made possible by the centrifugal force of boundless compassion. Such is the ultimate expansion and deepening of the bodhisattva ideal which breaks through conventional notions of time and space.

3

Progressive Stages of
Deep Hearing

Let us review the five stages more carefully. First, receptivity to the teaching means to receive the message
of the Larger Sutra, the principal scripture of the Pure
Land tradition. To receive means to hear, read, reflect,
discuss, question, and probe, whether by oneself or
in a group. As we do so, we come to appreciate the
working of the Primal Vow of Amida Buddha, the
boundless compassion directed to limited, finite beings, insuring their liberation from all kinds of karmic
bondages:

The word "hear" in the passage from the Larger Sutra means that sentient beings, having heard how the Buddha's Vow arose—its origin and fulfillment—are altogether free of doubt. This is to hear.[1]

Deep hearing has a twofold purpose. First is to awaken to the human condition as articulated in the Four Noble Truths of Shakyamuni Buddha, not as dogma but as the lived experience in everyday life. We thus come to realize ourselves as foolish beings bound by our karmic limitations—foolish because we are imperfect, limited, fallible, vulnerable, fragile, and mortal. Yet we forget this fact and go on living unaware that we create our own sufferings; we blame others when life does not move according to our wishes. The second purpose of deep hearing is to awaken to the working of boundless compassion, whose sole mission is to liberate us from the binding karmic conditions, transforming pain and sorrow into deep insight and received wisdom. Such a transformation, available to everyone, is foundational to any grand social program for change and betterment of society.

The Primal Vow of the Buddha Amida was accomplished in timeless time to liberate all beings from the darkness of ignorance. This story, contained in the Larger Sutra, begins with the forty-eight vows of the Bodhisattva Dharmakara, the Buddha-to-be, who shouldered the burden of suffering humanity and vowed to meet every conceivable need, both material and spiritual, of sentient beings as the condition for attaining Buddhahood. When Dharmakara fulfilled all the vows and accomplished this, the result was the liberating message of NAMU-AMIDA-BUTSU. This story, couched in mytho-poetic terms, is not a story in the ordinary sense, nor is it about a happening in history that took place in some remote past and in some distant land. Rather, it is the truth of the Larger Sutra becoming realized in one's own life and shaping one's self-understanding. Having been confirmed and reconfirmed innumerable times by people, beyond any human recall, the story is the cumulative realization of countless human beings down through the centuries. The cause of human suffering—whether physical, material, social, or spiritual—is the blind passion arising from our ego-self, erupting as greed, hatred, and ignorance. It has roots much deeper than anything we can ever fathom by common sense or reasoning.

The reason we can't fathom the roots of suffering is that each of us carries the historical burdens of deceit, treachery, and violence committed by our forbears across ethnic, racial, and religious lines. When we are not aware of this burden, ignorance surfaces in our life at unexpected moments as unbearable ennui, inexplicable melancholy, or soulful depression. It is a perplexing phenomenon, for when we think we should be happy and content with our lives, we suddenly experience malcontent, dissatisfaction, and affliction. The Russians have a word for this, *toska,* and it appears in the writings of great Russian novelists. In Dostoevsky's *White Nights,* for example, one of the main characters says, "At the break of dawn, a strange *toska* began to torture me. It suddenly seemed to me that I was shunned by all."[2]

This phenomenon defies rational comprehension, but it is the concern of boundless compassion.

The Sanskrit word for compassion, *karuna,* connotes wailing, moaning, and groaning and thus shares an experience of human pain with *toska.* Such deep existential suffering demands an enormous amount of time, energy, and imagination to cope with it properly. This is the reason that Dharmakara Bodhisattva spent five and even ten kalpas (both suggesting inconceivable eons of time) to fulfill the forty-eight Vows of liberation and freedom. Thus, Shinran states:

> When I ponder on the compassionate Vow of Amida, established through five kalpas of profound thought, it was for myself, Shinran, alone. Because I am a being burdened so

heavily with karma, I feel even more deeply grateful to the Primal Vow that is made to decisively save me.[3]

Now, as we progress in deep hearing, a focused intensity occurs. Like a laser beam searching for its target, our listening becomes more pointed. This is what Hokei meant when he said, "Listen and grasp the one corner (*kado*), and everything becomes clear."[4] It is reminiscent of Confucius' description of a good student who grasps one corner and immediately understands the whole (Analects, VII:8).

When one thus relates to the Buddha Dharma, the unfolding awareness of its truths is confirmed in one's own life. That is, in the great tradition of Buddhist pragmatism, the teaching of the Buddha is tested as gold is tested by fire and is confirmed to one's total satisfaction, leaving not a shadow of a doubt as to its veracity. In terms of self-understanding, we are shown who and what we are in the light of Buddha Dharma. In Shin Buddhism, this means that every saying of the nembutsu makes us realize our fundamental, limited reality as *namu,* this lost, confused, and anxious self, secure within boundless compassion, *amida-butsu,* the Buddha of Immeasurable Light and Life. Each intoning of NAMU-AMIDA-BUTSU is a reminder of this fact.

In the process of deep hearing, the isolated *namu* realizes its oneness with *amida-butsu,* and our wholeness is affirmed as NAMU-AMIDA-BUTSU. In this realization, the transformation of darkness to light is an ongoing process, and the working of the Primal Vow of the Buddha is realized as an accomplished fact. As Alfred Bloom puts it, "The Nembutsu is not the means to salvation, but the witness or evidence of it. Its appearance is testimony that the Vow has actually been fulfilled."[5]

The third stage is the interplay of light and darkness, boundless compassion and blind passions. As we proceed in deep hearing, we see ever more clearly this interplay as "hearing the light."

This strange expression simply means that through deep hearing we become increasingly aware of our everyday reality as a never-ending drama of highs and lows, ups and downs, ego-inflation and deflation, moments of happiness and sadness, triumphs and defeats, pride and humility. The luminous compassion, all-embracing and nonjudgmental, reveals our reality as "floundering in the ocean of birth-and-death." A simple example of "floundering" occurs in the following event.

Some years ago a friend in Los Angeles told me about an incident that happened to her neighbor. He started his car in his driveway to go on an errand. Having forgotten something, he ran into the house, leaving the motor running. When he came out of the house, the car was gone. It had vanished. He immediately called the police to report a stolen vehicle. Distraught that someone had taken his car from his own driveway, he was angry and upset. But the next morning he found his car parked in his driveway. When he went to check it out, he saw a small white envelope on the dashboard. Contained in it was a note that read, "Sorry to have taken your car, but I had an emergency. My child got sick and I had to take him to the hospital. I had no other transportation, so I borrowed your car. As a token of my appreciation, here are two free tickets to the Los Angeles Dodgers ballgame this Saturday." The man and his wife went off to the baseball game that Saturday afternoon, delighted that he could be a good Samaritan for a change. But when they returned home, they discovered that their house had been ransacked and everything valuable had been taken.

This alternation of ups and downs—deflation because of the stolen car, inflation because of two free baseball tickets, again deflation because of the outright thievery—is what Buddhists call floundering in the ocean of birth-and-death. It reminds us of a well-known story from the Chinese about a peasant living in a northern province. He owned a horse, and one day it ran away. He was dejected and crestfallen, until a few days later the horse returned with several fine steeds. Then misfortune struck again, when his son rode one of the steeds, got thrown off, and broke his leg. The peasant got very upset but there was nothing that he could do. Soon thereafter a civil war engulfed his region, and all the young men were drafted. But his son was not drafted because of his broken leg. In the war nine out of ten young men died, but his son was safe.

The light of the compassionate Buddha illuminates our karmic reality as infinite finitude. This means that, as finite human beings, we can live forever in ignorance and darkness, unless and until our karmic reality is illuminated by the light of compassion. As one of my Buddhist professors once said, "No matter how smart a dog is, a dog is still a dog." When we acknowledge our human reality, the light of compassion begins to work a miraculous transformation, where we become more open and flexible and accepting of ourselves and others. This is the fourth stage.

When the call of nembutsu reaches us, the transformation of darkness into light, blind passions into enlightenment, takes place and leads to the flowering of true and real life. This transformation cannot be manipulated or forced; it happens naturally, like the ripening of fruit. The natural process of maturation gives the fruit a rich taste and texture, unlike the artificial process of ripening.

The fifth and final stage reminds us that this is not simply an internal, subjective process and underscores our responsibilities in society. We meet all kinds of challenges—personal, social, and historical—and we vigorously respond to them, knowing that there are no quick and easy solutions. But, using the wisdom granted us by boundless compassion, we respond creatively and effectively to deal with any situation, good or bad. Practically speaking, this means to grow as human beings by continually reliving the five stages—open receptivity to the Buddha Dharma, unfolding awareness of its relevance to one's life, affirming the interplay of light and darkness in our every thought, speech, and action, responding to the Name-that-calls in meeting every challenge, and maintaining the balance of humility and gratitude. This process leads to "transforming delusion into enlightenment" which comes by itself and of its own accord.

4

Beyond the

Psychological

The practice of deep hearing is more than psychological for two reasons. First, the process takes us beyond
the working of the self-absorbed, calculating mind,
beyond what is called *self-power.* Second, it is pursued
within a framework of boundless compassion that exceeds conceptual understanding, the invisible Other
Power. This broad religious framework is provided by
the Larger Sutra and is made available to us in encap-
sulated form as the Name, NAMU-AMIDA-BUTSU.

One of the liturgical forms in the Pure Land tradition that provides the context for engaging in deep hearing is the Five Gates of Contemplation, as stipulated by Vasubandhu of India (circa fourth century). The first gate is worship. When we bow and prostrate ourselves before the Buddha image, it is not just a physical act but includes the awareness that one is the only child of the Buddha. In the words of Genshin (942–1017), the sixth master of Pure Land tradition,

> The Buddha's regard for each sentient being with eyes of compassion is equal, as though each one were the Buddha's only child; hence I take refuge in and worship the unsurpassed mother of great compassion.[1]

The bowing with palms placed together is *namu* bowing to *amida-butsu,* but it is also NAMU–AMIDA–BUTSU together bowing to all of existence, affirming the vast web of interdependent and interconnected life.

This is followed by the second gate, praising the Light of boundless compassion. The light of compassion illuminates the dark shadow within each of us, but we focus not on darkness but on light. This light, moreover, is not a mere sliver, but it interpenetrates with billions and billions of lights that illuminate our universe. This efflorescence is described poetically as flowers that bloom and emit rays of light in the Pure Land. In the words of Shinran,

> *Beams of light, thirty-six hundred*
> *Thousand billion in number*
> *Shine brilliantly from within each flower—*
> *There is no place they do not reach.*[2]

This is another metaphor for the vast network of interdependence and interconnectedness that is our life.

The third gate is the aspiration for transcendence, the liberation from the darkness of ignorance (*avidya*) and the havoc created by our blind passions. Traditionally, this is called the "aspiration to be born in the Pure Land," the goal of which is to acquire the power and facility to save all beings.

The fourth gate is contemplating the glories of the Pure Land and the auspicious features of Amida Buddha. Both the glories and features are manifestations of the fundamental reality in Buddhism called "emptiness" (*shunyata*) which nullifies any substance or essence to phenomena. If fundamental reality is nonsubstantial and noncorporeal, then "emptiness" can express itself in any form, shape, or color. Such is the philosophical basis of understanding Pure Land and Amida Buddha.

The fifth gate is sharing the spiritual benefits thus gained with all beings, as aids on their path of enlightenment. In the world of interdependence and interconnectedness, self-benefit is benefiting others, and benefiting others is self-benefit. The goal of the bodhisattva path is to realize that the two are interrelated and that simultaneous fulfillment is none other than supreme enlightenment.

The practice of the Five Gates is likened to a person walking through a mansion. First, one approaches the entrance gate, then joins other people in the open courtyard. Next, one enters the main entrance to the mansion, then moves into the inner sanctuary, and finally exits from the rear to frolic in the back garden. This garden is the world of the bodhisattva who engages in the playful sport of self-benefiting and benefiting others, ultimately aiming for the liberation and freedom of all beings. According to Shinran,

And when they reach the lotus-held world,
They immediately realize the body of suchness or dharma-nature.

> *Then sporting in the forests of blind passions, they manifest*
> *transcendent powers;*
> *Entering the garden of birth-and-death, they assume various*
> *forms to guide others.*[3]

Now, the practice of deep hearing involves one's whole being, for the ultimate realization means to embody the teaching and integrate it into everyday life, thus going beyond mere doctrinal assent or intellectual comprehension. That this is central to Asian religions has been acknowledged by Christians who are familiar with both Eastern and Western cultures. Thus, the Sri Lankan Jesuit theologian Aloysius Pieris states: "It is common knowledge that the West *studies* all the world religions, whereas the East simply *practices* them."[4] Cardinal Paul Shan Kuohsi of Taiwan also alerted his Christian counterparts at the Synod of Asia: "Missionaries to Asia must keep in mind the cultural context that places much more emphasis on an experience of the divine than on the intellectual."[5]

We find this somatic stress central to the insightful dialogue on Buddhism held between a distinguished French scientist and philosopher, Jean-François Revel, and his son, Matthieu Ricard, in *The Monk and the Philosopher.*[6] Ricard, who himself was once a rising scientist, has been a monk in the Tibetan tradition for thirty years. He gives three reasons for the current Western interest in Buddhism. In brief, he states that it teaches a way to integrate a living system of metaphysics into one's life, it provides a vision of tolerance and a science of mind to enable inner peace to flower in both self and others, and it makes ideas available to anyone through the sharing of experiences. All three points are the products of Buddhist meditative and nonmeditative traditions, regardless of different schools and their varying emphases.

The optimum functioning of the body-mind unity is not restricted to the religious alone; it is at the core of ethical life as well as the aesthetic and artistic. The basis is self-cultivation (*shugyo*), which permeates East Asian cultures. The teacher of ethics, for example, must embody the principles that he teaches; he himself must lead an ethical life and set the example. The creative artist masters a craft through apprenticeship, unlearns bad habits of the body, and produces a work of art that manifests his or her total reality. Once, when Joshu Sasaki Roshi visited my office and saw my father's calligraphy, I said, "He wasn't a good calligrapher." Roshi immediately responded, "There is no good or bad in calligraphy, just so it manifests the person writing it."

Whether it be calligraphy, dance, archery, poetry, or other arts, this training is accomplished through mastery of proper *kata,* or "form." The idea of mastering form comes from the Noh theater, which originated in fourteenth-century Japan, whereby an actor-dancer undergoes a transformation that includes the following process: re-forming the body, con-forming to *kata,* and per-forming to one's maximum capability. When we fully comprehend this training of the body-mind unity, we can also appreciate the cryptic sayings of the famous Japanese potter Kanjiro Kawai, who sums up his craft with the words, "hand thinks, foot reflects" and "hand leads, foot aspires."[7]

In self-cultivation the burden of learning is on the student. Instructions are all nonverbal; keen observation and intuition become central. This requires will power, perseverance, and commitment; it becomes a test of character. As a consequence, the goal is secondary, and the process is everything. In focusing on a process that requires patience and fortitude, the body and mind undergo a transformation in order to manifest optimum functioning.

This tradition of self-cultivation forms the unseen background of the Shin Buddhist life, which shuns theoretical discussions and encourages people to embody the teachings. In the course of deep hearing, a transformation of body and mind, conscious and subconscious, takes place in subtle and unknown ways. The understanding of the teaching moves from the cognitive level to the subconscious level, where the sedimentation of the Buddha's teaching occurs in the deepest layers of the psyche. This ultimately leads to the rigid self becoming supple, flexible, and open. In the words of Shinran, "That all have their bodies touched by the light is due to the working of the 'Vow of softness and gentleness of body and mind.' "[8]

5

Religion and

Spirituality

Today we frequently hear people say, "I'm not interested in religion; I'm interested only in spirituality."
When people speak of religion, the reference is usu-
ally to its historical manifestations: the institutions
with their ecclesiastical hierarchy, elaborate rituals,
creeds, dogmas, paternalism, and subtle psychic violence often inflicted on their members. In contrast,
spirituality suggests liberation from the binding con-
straints of institutional religion and the freedom to
seek solace in whatever form one finds it, whether it

be in nature, cultic practices, out-of-body experiences, or popularized versions of Eastern religions and philosophies.

According to Martin Marty, the distinguished historian of American religion, who gave a lecture on this topic at Smith College a few years ago, both are needed in today's world. Religion needs a dose of spirituality to give it vigor, and spirituality can use religion to give it structure and form. While structure and form, embodied in traditional religious liturgy and worship, may not appeal to those brought up in our New Age culture, they are necessary, I believe, for the nourishment and development of true religiosity, for two reasons.

First, true religious life involves not only the conscious self but the irrational, unconscious self, which has the potential of unleashing powerful emotions. These emotions need to be channeled in creative ways, and traditional rituals have served that purpose. Carl Jung speaks positively of dogmas as being superior to science because they once dealt with the irrational. In his words, dogma "expresses the living process of the unconscious in the form of the drama of repentance, sacrifice, and redemption."[1]

Second, rituals handed down through the centuries provide a stabilizing ground to the emotional fluctuations that are our common lot, whether religious or nonreligious. Like the weather in New England, emotional states constantly undergo change without any warning. We thus yearn to become connected to something enduring and consistent. This is where devotional sutra-chanting in Buddhism plays a crucial role. No matter what one's psychological state may be, communal chanting provides a soothing setting that cannot be easily created by any other means.

The ritual of sutra chanting, whether communal or individual, also connects us to a practice that goes back thousands of years and includes diverse settings. In my own case, the number of Shin Buddhists in New England is minuscule, but I am part of a larger Shin Sangha in space and time. My chanting resonates with the chanting by Shin Buddhists across the globe, in Kyoto, Honolulu, Anchorage, San Francisco, Chicago, Boston, London, Antwerp, Dusseldorf, Salzburg, Geneva, Kenya, Rio de Janeiro, Sydney, Singapore, and Hong Kong. It also connects me to my childhood, when we had daily chanting before the home altar, and to my father's temple in Kyushu, Japan, where early morning and evening chanting had been conducted for twelve generations at the same site. But it goes even further back, to the oral transmissions from the time of the historical Buddha in India in the fifth century B.C.E.

The contemporary significance of sutra chanting is expressed by the poet Cathy Song, who participates in daily group chanting of the *Shoshinge* (The Hymn of True Entrusting), composed by Shinran, at the Buddhist Study Center in Honolulu. Here is her poem, entitled "Fetters":

Every morning I come to Shoshinge.
Every morning it is the same.

Between my mind and the mind of compassion,
Amida Buddha's wisdom and light,
the hymn flutters like a veil.
All is settled.
All is well.

I am the recipient of all that is settled.
Of all that is well.
I long to enter the veil,
I give up my voice,
coarse, thick phlegm stone of sleep,
to meet the infinite
bountifulness with breath
moments of faith.

Every morning it is the same.
All is settled.
All is well.
I long to enter the veil.

I open my mouth, a cave
blackened with the smoke of desire.
I open my throat to lift
stone from breath and push
what falls firm
in the heavy tide of night.

My sorrowing heart staggers into sunlight
drunk with complaints,
easily distracted,
burdened and unsettled.
It waits.

Sing, practice, surrender!
All is assured
but my heart, blindfolded, attaches
disappointments, pins grievances
upon the veil like a child
spinning in circles, left
holding the donkey's tail.

I fling my worries upon the veil,
a tangled web of fetters.
Cluttered heart!
So disorderly and rude!

Every morning I come to Shoshinge.
Every morning it is the same.[2]

The *Shoshinge* is a summation of the basic scriptures of Pure Land Buddhism and the teachings of the seven masters of Shin Buddhism, which include Nagarjuna and Vasubandhu of India, T'an-luan, Tao-ch'o and Shan-tao of China, and Genshin and Honen of Japan.[3]

6

Primal Vow

The story of Dharmakara Bodhisattva is not a story in the ordinary sense, for it articulates the maturing process of a religious seeker. That is, it shapes the inner quest of the seeker as he or she engages in deep hearing, transforming the story found in the Larger Sutra into one's personal history. Moreover, the story contains the cumulative experience of countless human beings down through the centuries, giving it a richness and substance beyond the merely personal. In an important early work on women and religion, *Womanspirit Rising: A Feminist Reader in Religion,* Carol Christ and Judith Plaskow write that "There is a dialectic between stories and experience. Stories shape experience, and experience shapes stories."[1] This statement is helpful for us in appreciating the genesis of the Primal Vow of Dharmakara Bodhisattva and its fulfillment in the attainment of Buddhahood. What do we mean by this?

We begin with a little story written by Gary Snyder, the Pulitzer Prize-winning poet, who gives us a sense of what people might have thought when giving shape and form to an elemental religious experience. In an essay called "Who the Buddhas Are," he writes:

All the beings of the universe are already realized. That is, with the exception of one or two beings. In those rare cases the cities, villages, meadows, and forests, with all their birds, flowers, animals, rivers, trees, and humans, that surround such a person, all collaborate to educate, serve, challenge, and instruct such a one, until that person also becomes a New Beginner Enlightened Being. Recently realized beings are enthusiastic to teach and train and start schools and practices. Being able to do this develops their confidence and insight up to the point that they are fully ready to join the seamless world of interdependent play. Such new enlightened beginners are called the "Buddhas" and they like to say things like, "I am enlightened together with the whole universe" and so forth.[2]

Various factors that constitute the Primal Vow are found here. That "all beings of the universe are already realized" is the basic assumption of the Buddhist path. Thus, all of animate and inanimate existence conspire to awaken each person to the highest, unexcelled enlightenment. The paradigm of such an awakening is Dharmakara Bodhisattva, who attains Buddhahood. His Primal Vow of universal emancipation enters the "seamless world of interdependent play" in order to engage in salvific activities for all beings. It brings to reality the foundational promise, "I am enlightened together with the whole universe."

That not a single person is left out of this grand scheme necessarily means that the Primal Vow must be concerned, above all else, with the lowest of lowliest beings—those abandoned, neglected, forgotten, those living in the darkness of ignorance, those unable to deal with their blind passions and addictions. They become the focus of the working of the Primal Vow, ultimately bringing about a transformation that enables them to become liberated and free. In due course of time this focus evolved into the narrative of the Larger Sutra that is summed up in the Eighteenth Vow, the Primal Vow, of Bodhisattva Dharmakara, which proclaims:

> If, when I attain Buddhahood, the sentient beings of the ten quarters, with sincere mind, entrusting themselves, aspiring to be born in my land, and saying my Name perhaps even ten times, should not be born there, may I not attain the supreme enlightenment. Excluded are those who commit the five grave offenses and those who slander the dharma.[3]

That the exclusion clause is contained in the vow of enlightenment is significant, for it underscores the primary object of great compassion. That is, on one level it is an ethical injunction warning against committing the offenses—hurting mother, father, and monk; injuring the Buddha; and destroying the Sangha—and slandering the Dharma, but on a deeper level it highlights the very object of nonexclusive compassion: the abandoned, confused, lost, and deluded person.[4]

Although the Primal Vow did not appear in scripture until much later in the history of Buddhism, its primordial form can be found in early Buddhism. We can feel the faint stirrings of the Primal Vow in the famous parable of the mustard seed from the time of the historical Buddha. A young mother in deep grief, Kisa Gotami, had lost her only child and went to Shakyamuni Buddha to request medicine to bring him back to life. She had already experienced the death of several members of her family, including her husband. When Gotami, known as the Frail One (*kisa*), pleaded with the Buddha, he promised to give her the medicine if she would only go into the village, get a handful of mustard seeds, and bring them back to him. But there was one condition: the mustard seeds must come from a household that had never known death.

Kisa Gotami rushed off to beg for a handful of mustard seeds. Every household was willing to give her some, but no matter where she turned, every family had known death—the painful loss of a father, a sister, a son, an aunt, a mother, a brother, an uncle, and so on without end. Confronting this universal human tragedy, Kisa Gotami's personal vow to bring her little boy back to life awakened her to a larger, universal vow—the Primal Vow that assures liberation and freedom for all beings—in which mother and son both come truly alive in a real, enduring form. Her grief at the loss of her son opened up the horizon of compassionate concern coming from the center of life itself. Kisa Gotami's personal prayer is expressive of a much deeper and more capacious prayer, the Primal Vow of Amida, which liberates all beings from their karmic bondage.[5]

In this parable we see personal grief becoming a medium through which one feels the working of boundless compassion that focuses on the most vulnerable, the neediest, the weakest. Deep hearing awakens us to the Primal Vow surging within each of us, and we experience vividly Amida's compassion in our own lives. It is the channel through which boundless compassion reaches us, since the auditory is the most receptive of sense faculties. We have some choice regarding the other senses—to see or not see, taste or not taste, touch or not touch, and smell or not smell—but we have no such choice regarding hearing. We can cover our ears with our hands or ear plugs, but the sound of the Name-that-calls never ceases ringing in our ears.

It is noteworthy that the original character for "hear" in Chinese and Japanese consists of two parts: the ideograph for "gate" which contains that for "ear." This for me means that hearing is the gate to the spiritual life. When we hear the call of boundless compassion, we are already on the path to supreme enlightenment. Hearing is also the essential quality of the bodhisattva of compassion, Kuan-yin or Kannon, who responds to the needy upon hearing the mournful cries and plaintive laments of suffering beings in the world.

Religiously speaking, deep hearing means that we have no choice but to hear and respond to the call of boundless compassion. It is through the Name-that-calls that Amida Buddha gives us the ultimate gift of true and real life. The invisible Other Power is not an abstract concept, nor is it a metaphysical agent, but it is the dynamism of the vital life awakening us and invigorating us. Thus, the invocation of the Name, NAMU–AMIDA–BUTSU, is not just a simple act of religious piety but a voicing of the call that comes from the bottomless source of life itself, the Buddha of Immeasurable Light and Life. My good friend Edith, a former school principal, discerns the source of nembutsu in relation to her own inadequate utterance:

Hands together in gassho,
Only empty nembutsu seem

> *To gush out of my mouth.*
> *Yet to my amazement*
> *Out of this emptiness comes*
> *Amida's call—just as you are,*
> *Just as you are.*
> NAMU–AMIDA–BUTSU.[6]

Edith's saying of NAMU–AMIDA–BUTSU joins the chorus of countless enlightened beings all praising the Name, their voices reverberating in countless universes in the ten directions.

Rainer Maria Rilke once remarked about the Buddha sitting in his garden to this friend Rodin, "*C'est le centre du monde* [He is the center of the world]."[7] He then composed the poem entitled "The Buddha in the Glory":

> *Center of centers, core of cores*
> *almond self-enclosed and growing sweet—*
> *all this universe, to the furthest stars*
> *and beyond them, is your flesh, your fruit.*
>
> *Now you feel how nothing clings to you;*
> *your vast shell reaches into endless space,*
> *and there the rich, thick fluids rise and flow.*
> *Illuminated in our infinite space.*
>
> *A billion stars go spinning through the night,*
> *blazing high above your head.*
> *But in you is the presence that*
> *will be, when all the stars are dead.*[8]

Like the almond, the Primal Vow is the center of centers, ever expanding and ever growing. Its essential spirit fills the universe, carrying the burdens of suffering humanity, reaching fulfillment, and bringing about the fruit in endless space. The working of the Primal Vow will continue throughout the upheavals and travails of human history, never ending as "something which longer than the suns shall burn."[9]

7

The Absolute Present

At the end of 1999, when the world was filled with anxiety about Y2K and the coming millennium, I was asked by a Christian theologian to write a short article on the New Millennium from the Buddhist standpoint. I had to decline, since the millennium may have significance for those who believe in the Second Coming as prophesied in the Book of Revelations, but it has no special significance for a Buddhist who is a nontheist. As the Dalai Lama said, "For me it is nothing, New Millennium, New Century, New Year. For me it is another day and night. The sun, the moon, the stars remain the same."¹ My friend, however, persisted, so I decided to write on some Japanese Buddhist customs relating to the New Year observance.

For a Buddhist every year is a New Year, every day a New Day, and every moment a New Moment. The significance of life is to be discovered in the here and now, not in some remote past nor in some unknown future. But this realization does not come easily, for we live in a linguistically constructed world where clock time, calendar time, and abstract time are easily mistaken for Time itself.

A common practice on New Year's Eve throughout Japan is for people to go to a Buddhist temple and strike the huge temple gong 108 times. It is a reminder that we are bound by 108 delusions that hinder our ability to see things, including the self, as they are. The number 108 was a popular number in ancient India and is based on the multiple sources of our delusions. They include the five senses, plus the mind, which misperceive reality as it is, totaling six delusions; the six objects of perception, whether desirable, undesirable, or neither, and whether pleasurable, not pleasurable, or neither, causing six more delusions. When they are combined and multiplied, thirty-six misperceptions occur; and when they are multiplied by the three time periods of past, present, and future, the grand total comes to 108 delusions.

While past, present, and future are human constructs that are helpful and convenient, they have nothing to do with reality as it is. They are verbal constructs that abound in our life, similar to the constructs we use everyday—good and bad, right and left, East and West, big and small, black and white, *ad infinitum*. They are useful and generally necessary but have only conventional value; when we fail to see this and mistake words for reality, we weave a world of delusions. Henry Wadsworth Longfellow critiques the conventional notion of time:

What is time? The shadow on the dial, the striking of a clock, the running of the sand, day and night, summer and winter, months, years, centuries—these are but arbitrary and natural signs, the measure of Time, not Time itself. Time is the life of the soul.[2]

According to Buddhism, constant change, flux, and impermanence are the very basis of life. Our life is a series of micromoments that we never notice, because the shortest unit of time—one-sixtieth of the time it takes to snap your fingers—cannot be seen by the naked eye. It is as though we are entranced by an old movie unfolding on the screen, unaware that each frame that makes up the film is separate and distinct. On the screen of life we assume continuity, but the reality is that the film can stop at any frame, freeze at any instant. The continuum is a delusion.

Actual lived time, Time itself, flows below conventional notions of time, whether clock time, calendar time, or abstract time. This is what Longfellow means when he says, "Time is the life of the soul." A story is told of Te-shan Hsuan-chien as a young Zen monk, traveling from monastery to monastery in medieval China. He comes to a rest stop for a refreshing cup of tea. A little old woman comes out to serve him and notices that he has the *Diamond Sutra* in his hand. Recalling a famous passage from the sutra, she quotes, "The past mind cannot be grasped, the future mind cannot be grasped, and the present mind cannot be grasped," and then asks, "Sir, which mind do you want to refresh?"[3] Unable to answer, Te-shan burns his books and begins his serious quest for Zen attainment.

What is past has disappeared and cannot be grasped; the future, of course, has yet to come and cannot be grasped; and the present eludes our grasp because the moment we try to get hold of it, it is already in the past. The immediacy of the moment leaves no room for word play or conceptual dalliance. The living moment, here and now, demands our immediate and fullest attention. No longer concerned with the past, whether to be celebrated or regretted, nor with the future, whether to be anticipated with hope or apprehension, one lives fully and totally in the present. Thus, this chronological present is also a "present," a gift that must be opened, so that its rich content may be savored. In the words of the Zen master Dogen, each present is a moment of total dynamic life:

> Life is not a coming and it is not a going; it is not an existing
> and it is not a becoming. Nevertheless, life is the manifestation
> of the total dynamic working; death is the manifestation of the
> total dynamic working.[4]

In total dynamic working there is neither before nor after, neither life nor death.

This moment, however, is to be sharply distinguished from the emphasis on the here and now in ordinary discourse, such as found in the familiar saying "Eat, drink, and be merry, for tomorrow we die." This hedonistic cry stresses the importance of the moment, but it is empty and fraught with anxiety, containing a tinge of fatalism. It is just another form of nihilistic self-indulgence, disconnected from Time itself.

In contrast, an appreciation of Time is found in the art of tea ceremony. Its basic philosophy is epitomized in the aphorism: "a whole lifetime in a single encounter" (*ichigo-ichiye*). This Buddhist phrase suggests that each human encounter is more than purely accidental; in fact, it has deep roots in our karmic past and has vast implications in our interconnected and interdependent universe. The gathering for tea ceremony, normally limited to four or five guests, is a ritual of silence, underscored by the soft rolling murmur of boiling water and the faint sound of the whisking of powdered tea. All the movements are fluid and natural, coming from the centrum of *ki,* or *ch'i.* The five senses are heightened, and at-

tention is focused on the moment, this moment never to be repeated in eternity. Even if the same people should gather at the
same time on the following day, it would be an entirely different
experience. In life every moment awaits to be newly explored, for
a whole lifetime may be invested into a single moment. The host
offers a cup of tea, imbued with years of aesthetic accomplish-
ments, and the guest receives the cup of tea, not only with the
hands but with the total sincerity of one's whole being.

We find such significance of the moment, touched by the
timeless, in T. S. Eliot's *Burnt Norton,* describing the graceful
movements of a ballerina:

> *At the still point of the turning world. Neither flesh nor*
> *   fleshless;*
> *Neither from nor towards; at the still point, there the dance*
> *   is,*
> *But neither arrest nor movement. And do not call it fixity,*
> *Where past and future are gathered. Neither movement*
> *   from nor towards,*
> *Neither ascent nor decline. Except for the point, the still*
> *   point,*
> *There would be no dance, and there is only the dance,*
> *I can only say, there we have been: but I cannot say where,*
> *And I cannot say, how long, for that is to place it in time.*[5]

"The still point of the turning world" is the moment both
in and out of time. It is the intersection of the horizontal, linear
time of our everyday world and the vertical, timeless time of religious awakening which penetrates every instant of conventional
time.

How the two planes or dimensions intersect in one's life is illustrated by the reflections contained in the recent best-seller
Tuesdays with Morrie. The author, Mitch Albom, records the final
days of his former teacher, Morrie Schwartz, who is dying of Lou

Gehrig's disease, the gradual wasting away of nerves and muscles. A retired sociology professor at Brandeis University, Morrie laments that so many people walk around with a meaningless life, when they should be asking themselves: "Is this all? Is this all I want? Is something missing?"[6] Then he refers to Buddhism and suggests,

> "Do what the Buddhists do. Every day, have a little bird on your shoulder that asks, 'Is today the day? Am I ready? Am I doing all I need to do? Am I being the person I want to be?' " He turned his head to his shoulder as if the bird were there now. "Is today the day I die?" he said.[7]

This is not a morbid obsession with death and dying but a contemplative reflection on our life that will never return in eternity. The emphasis is on living here and now. In other words,

> To know you're going to die, and to be *prepared* for it at any time. That's better. That way you can actually be *more* involved in your life while you're living.[8]

The involvement in life here and now, cherishing each unrepeatable moment, is demanded of us especially when the end of linear time is fast approaching. This awakening may also occur when debilitating illness becomes a liberating experience: "If you are ill, you can experience more freedom to be who you really are and want to be because you now have nothing to lose."[9]

When future concerns on the horizontal plane of life become devoid of any meaning, shattered by terminal illness or imminent death, one is forced to turn to the depth dimension of reality here and now. If one has been exposed to some structure or framework of vertical awakening, religious or philosophical, then coping with uncertainties should be that much easier, even though no less painful. But it must be more than some form of abstraction; it must be realistically appropriated while we are relatively healthy and in good spirits.

Every funeral rite in Shin Buddhism reminds us of the intersection of horizontal and vertical dimensions. The convergence of the two comes in the form of an epistle read at such services, entitled "On White Ashes." Originally written by Rennyo (1415–1499), who rebuilt the Shin order of Hongwanji into a major religious force, we read:

In silently contemplating the transient nature of human existence, nothing in our world is more fragile and fleeting than our life. Thus, we hear of no one sustaining a human form for a thousand years. Life swiftly passes and who among us can maintain our human form for even a hundred years?

Whether I go before others, or others go before me; whether it be today, or it be tomorrow, who is to know? Those who leave before us are as countless as the drops of dew. Though in the morning we may have radiant health, in the evening we may return to ashes. When the winds of impermanence blow, our eyes are closed forever; and when the last breath leaves us, our face loses its color.

Though loved ones gather and lament, everything is to no avail. The body is then sent into an open field and vanishes from this world with the smoke of cremation, leaving only white ashes. There is nothing more real than this truth of life. The fragile nature of human existence underlies both the young and old, and therefore we must, one and all, turn to the teachings of the Buddha and awaken to the ultimate source of life.

By so understanding the meaning of death, we shall come to fully appreciate the meaning of this life which is unrepeatable and thus to be treasured above all else. By virtue of true compassion, let us realize the irreplaceable value of human life and let us together live the nembutsu in our hearts.[10]

Although written in the fifteenth century for unlettered followers in the countryside of northern Japan, the message is timeless and still speaks to us today. It reminds us of life's fragility as well as its preciousness, moment by moment, which must not be wasted. Morrie Schwartz sums up this elemental truth in a collection of his sayings, *Letting Go*: "When you learn how to live, you know how to die; when you learn how to die, you know how to live."[11]

8

Time at Its Ultimate Limit

According to Shinran, religious awakening is the realization of timeless time in each moment of temporal activity. The ultimate dimension breaks into the historical dimension, the timeless penetrates time. In his words, "One thought-moment is time at its ultimate limit, where the realization of shinjin takes place."[1] What does this mean? What is the ultimate limit of time? What does *shinjin,* or true entrusting, mean? What kind of awareness is it?

The "one thought-moment" underscores the irreplaceable, ultimate value of the here and now. It is the moment when vertical time breaks through into horizontal or linear time, the absolute penetrating the relative. In Buddhist discourse it is also the moment of formless reality, called *dharmakaya*, appearing as the Primal Vow of Amida in human consciousness.

The Primal Vow contains the deepest aspiration of countless enlightened beings down through human history, the aspiration that all beings shall attain perfect peace, happiness, and fulfillment. It has been fulfilled in the timeless past, and as such it has been pursuing us from the beginningless beginning of time. And the Pure Land in the future is the promise already fulfilled that all beings, no matter who they are, will achieve consummate awakening. The Primal Vow in the past and the Pure Land in the future, the alpha and omega of Shin religious life, are realized here and now in this "one thought-moment."[2]

One thought-moment is experienced in a twofold manner. One thought-moment of shinjin is the awakening to the Primal Vow in one's life, whereby all calculation has ceased and all doubts have vanished. It is a kind of awakening when one becomes free of the blind fetters of ignorance, reality as-it-is is affirmed, and true entrusting results as the working of the Primal Vow. Simultaneously, the utterance of nembutsu in one thought-moment is, the invocation of NAMU-AMIDA-BUTSU pouring out spontaneously as the vocal expression of total and joyful entrusting to the working of the Primal Vow. The two are interdependent and inseparable.

The new sense of life, imbued with timeless reality and the working of boundless compassion, is expressed variously by Shin practitioners. About a century ago in Japan, Saichi, the *myokonin* (nembutsu practitioner), wrote several poems alluding to this awakening. While pursuing his menial task everyday, the vertical plane intersected with his life on the horizontal plane at every point:

No need to wait for my end,
My end is no longer my concern.
What joy, compassion cares for me,
And I go to the land of bliss.
This self destined to die
Is made into NAMU-AMIDA-BUTSU
That never dies.[3]

Saichi goes to the Pure Land here and now, and he never dies, because he manifests the Primal Vow as he lives out his karmic life on the horizontal plane.

A devout Shin practitioner in the early twentieth century, Mitsuyo Makinodan of Hawaii, also left many songs of her nembutsu life where the horizontal and vertical intersect. Among her many poems, she writes:

Embraced by the light of Amida
My life that is fragile
As the morning dew
Now lives forever.[4]

The fragile life, destined to disappear, "now lives forever," for one lives rooted in the vertical dimension, the Primal Vow of boundless compassion.

Such an experience of time was the basis of Shinran's reinterpretation of "birth in the Pure Land," changing its original futuristic connotation into a radical affirmation of the here and now. He interprets the scripture that states, "Then they attain birth," to suggest an immediacy not apparent in the original. Thus, in his commentary, Shinran states: "*Then* means immediately; 'immediately' means without any passage of time, without any passage of days."[5]

Historically, for over a thousand years, the Pure Land symbolized various ideals of the religious life. Foremost among them was

the representation of the perfect realm to pursue the path of enlightenment, unobstructed by the din, commotion, and entanglements of our samsaric world. It was also the place to which the
dying would be welcomed by Amida Buddha and his retinue of
bodhisattvas coming down from the sky. In fact, a deathbed ritual
was developed in medieval Japan to insure successful birth into the
Pure Land. A folding screen with a painting of Amida Buddha,
looking down from among mountain peaks, was placed above the
bed of the dying person. A string attached to the heart of Amida
would be extended and firmly grasped by the dying, so that there
would be no chance of getting lost on the way to the Pure Land.

Shinran rejected this popular deathbed ritual as causing greater
anxiety about death and dying, as well as revealing a lack of trust
in the Primal Vow. He states:

> The idea of Amida's coming at the moment of death is for
> those who seek to gain birth in the Pure Land by perform-
> ing religious practices, for they are the practicers of self-
> power. The moment of death is of central concern for such
> people. . . . The person of true shinjin, however, abides in
> the stage of the truly settled, for he has already been grasped,
> never to be abandoned. There is no need to wait in antici-
> pation for the moment of death, no need to rely on Amida's
> coming. At the time shinjin becomes settled, birth too be-
> comes settled; there is no need for deathbed rites that pre-
> pare one for Amida's coming.[6]

There is no need for such a deathbed ritual, because birth in
the Pure Land has occurred in the awakening to shinjin here and
now. Hence, this awakening is also called the stage of the truly settled; there is no need to go seeking elsewhere. It is also described
as the rank of nonretrogression; there is no fear of backsliding to
earlier states of anxiety.

9

Shinjin as

True Entrusting

Shinjin is a kind of trust where doubt is nonexistent and assertion of any kind is unnecessary. It is different from the popular notions of "faith," which contain a vast range of meanings, mostly based on a dualistic view that focuses on an object outside of oneself. We believe that it is more appropriate to use words taken from ordinary life to translate *shinjin* into English, words such as "trust, confidence, steadfastness, certainty," that do not involve any kind of duality.

Since the timeless Primal Vow of Amida Buddha comes from the heart of boundless compassion, Alfred Bloom calls it "endowed trust." Since it also has nothing to do with the fickle mind of human beings, I use "true entrusting," an entrusting that is made possible by that which is true and real, namely, Amida Buddha.

To justify the distinction between faith and shinjin, Dennis Hirota speaks of two levels of engagement with Amida and Pure Land: initial and mature. In the initial engagement, both Amida and Pure Land are regarded as objects, dualistically conceived, but in mature engagement, they become an integral part of a fundamental awakening, such that the practitioner and Amida/Pure Land are experienced as nondual reality.[1]

The primary goal of Shin Buddhism is life lived in mature engagement with the Buddha Dharma. The ultimate goal of deep hearing is not satori or enlightenment but true entrusting. In the words of Shinran,

> For the foolish and ignorant who are ever sinking in birth-and-death, the multitude turning in transmigration, it is not attainment of the unexcelled, incomparable fruit of enlightenment that is difficult; the genuine difficulty is realizing true and real shinjin.[2]

The "genuine difficulty" comes from our deep-rooted self-clinging that will not open up to "true and real shinjin" that is the unconditional gift of boundless compassion. Shinran describes true and real shinjin variously: as diamond-like, because it is not dependent on the ego-self and hence is indestructible; as the settled state, because it is not subject to our emotional upheavals; and as nonretrogression, because there is no backsliding into confusion and darkness. Toward the end of his life, Shinran called shinjin a state *equal* to the Tathagata or Buddha; that is, it is not identical with Buddhahood but equals it, since supreme enlightenment will be attained necessarily as its natural consequence.

In carefully interpreting the writings of past masters of the Pure Land tradition from his own experiential reading, Shinran concluded that the three basic attitudes stipulated in the Eighteenth Vow—sincere mind, joyful entrusting, and aspiration for the Pure Land—can be unified as the single heart-mind of Amida working in foolish beings to bring about true entrusting. Traditionally, this is called Three Minds as the working of a Single Mind.

In brief, the Single Mind unfolds in the following manner. "Sincere mind" denotes the mind of the Buddha and not that of ordinary beings. It enters the deluded minds of foolish, ignorant beings, making it possible for them to experience a "joyful entrusting" to the working of boundless compassion. This in turn awakens the thought of transcending the world of delusion, that is, "aspiring for the Pure Land," so that one may acquire the wisdom and compassion necessary to work for the salvation of all beings.

Shinran also interpreted the Three Minds in the Contemplation Sutra in the light of the above reading. He concluded that the Three Minds in the Contemplation Sutra differ only on the surface, for their implicit meaning corroborates the explicit meaning found in the Three Minds expounded in the Larger Sutra.

The Three Minds of the Contemplation Sutra are sincere mind, deep mind, and the mind of aspiration for birth that includes the transference of the acquired benefits to others. Here again the sincere mind refers to the true and real mind of Amida Buddha and not the mind of sentient beings "filled with all manner of greed, anger, perversity, deceit, wickedness, and cunning." Deep mind involves two kinds of awareness:

Deep mind is the deeply entrusting mind. There are two aspects. One is to believe deeply and decidedly that you are a foolish being of karmic evil caught in birth-and-death, ever sinking and ever wandering in transmigration from innumerable kalpas in the past, with never a condition that would lead to emancipation. The second is to believe deeply and decidedly that Amida Buddha's Forty-eight vows grasp sentient beings, and that allowing yourself to be carried by the power of the Vow without any doubt or apprehension, you will attain birth.[3]

The working of sincere mind results not only in true entrusting but also inspires a person to aspire for transcendence, to go beyond this world of suffering in order to gain the wisdom and compassion to save beings floundering in the ocean of birth-and-death.

Shinran analyzes carefully the meanings of each of the three minds, for they have multiple connotations which give them a rich texture describing human experience. After listing the synonyms for "sincere" (truth, reality) and "mind" (seed, kernel), Shinran concludes:

> We see clearly that sincere mind is the mind that is the seed of truth, reality, and sincerity; hence, it is completely untainted by the hindrance of doubt.[4]

He then proceeds to sum up the synonyms for "true" and "entrusting" and states:

> Entrusting is the mind full of truth, reality, and sincerity; the mind of ultimacy, accomplishment, reliance, and reverence; the mind of discernment, distinctness, clarity, and faithfulness; the mind of aspiration, wish, desire, and exultation; the mind of delight, joy, gladness, and happiness; hence it is completely untainted by doubt.[5]

Finally, he clarifies the multiple meanings of "aspiration" and "birth":

> Aspiration for birth is the mind of wish, desire, awakening, and awareness; the mind of accomplishment, fulfillment, performance, and establishment. It is the mind of great compassion directing itself to beings; hence, it is completely untainted by the hindrance of doubt.[6]

Shinran thus concludes his linguistic analysis and states: "The Tathagata gives this sincere mind to all living things, an ocean of beings possessed of blind passions, karmic evil, and false wisdom. This mind manifests the true mind of benefiting others. For this reason, it is completely untainted by the hindrance of doubt. This sincere mind takes as its essence the revered Name of supreme virtues."[7]

Shinran frequently uses the expression "returning to the ocean of the Primal Vow" for shinjin. He likens it to the great ocean that does not discriminate between good and bad, young and old, men and women, noble and humble. Nor does it differentiate between practitioner and nonpractitioner, sudden and gradual attainment, right and wrong contemplation, once-calling and many-calling. The working of shinjin is ultimately

> inconceivable, inexplicable, and indescribable. It is like the medicine that eradicates all poisons. The medicine of the Tathagata's Vow destroys the poison of our wisdom and foolishness.[8]

When we think that we have attained some kind of wisdom, it is nothing but arrogance, and as such it poisons ourselves and those around us. Only the medicine of nembutsu can eradicate such a toxic condition. But just as an ordinary person does not know the base chemicals in a prescription medicine yet derives good from it, so likewise the practitioner of the Shin path cannot fathom the depth of nembutsu life yet receives inconceivable benefits from it.

10

A Path Less Taken

The popular view is that all religions are in essence the same; they are but different paths to the mountaintop. This may be true for a detached observer or a student of religious studies, but if you seek to reach the mountaintop, you must choose one path and commit yourself to that path. Otherwise, you will be scrambling all over the mountain slope, hurting yourself in the process and never reaching the top.

It is not a matter of one path being superior to another; rather, it is a question of which path suits one's needs, abilities, and temperament. The same holds true, for example, in selecting a wardrobe. When you walk into a clothing store, the choices are countless. In the men's shop all the suits are the same, in spite of variations in color and size and style. Objectively speaking, any distinction among them is inconsequential if you are just looking, but if you wish to buy one, you must choose the one that fits you and pay for it. Even if you are attracted to a particular suit for its color or its style, unless the size is right, it is useless.

According to Pure Land masters, there are two paths to the mountaintop of liberation and freedom from the fetters of samsaric life. Traditionally, they are called the path of Sages and the path of Pure Land, a distinction first made by the Chinese master Tao-ch'o in the early seventh century. The path of Sages is a generic term for the monastic traditions that constitute the major schools of Buddhism. This path requires renunciation of family, society, and all worldly ties, and a commitment to celibacy, poverty, innumerable precepts, and demanding disciplines.

The path of Pure Land, on the other hand, is primarily a way for the laity; it is available to any one, regardless of status, who seeks the path of enlightenment. This path is for people engaged in raising a family, making a living, doing productive work, negotiating through life's endless demands. In traditional Asia such people also provided material support for the monks and nuns, so that the latter could fulfill their religious vocations. This path of Pure Land is also known as the Straight Way, a direct and unobstructed path to liberation and freedom, due to the working of boundless compassion, in contrast to the path of Sages, which can be circuitous, full of obstacles, temptations, and pitfalls.

The current Western interest in Buddhism focuses primarily on the path of Sages; especially attractive are the great variety of meditative practices not found in Western religions, such as Zen, Tibetan Buddhism, and Vipassana. This path seems to appeal to those who seek self-development, self-esteem, self-confidence, self-expression, self-control, and that is fine, but one must also know that this is contrary to the goal of Buddhist practice. As Mark Epstein correctly puts it, "In Buddhism, the impenetrable, separate, and individuated self is more of the problem than a solution."[1] But no-self (*anatta, anatman*) does not simply mean the obliteration of the self; rather, it is *attachment* to the fiction of self that is to be negated.

When Americans flock to Zen retreats, Tibetan Buddhist centers, and Vipassana training sessions, they are no longer strictly monastic, for the practices are modified to meet the needs of people who pursue their own professional or private secular lives. This diluted form of the path of Sages has both positive and negative consequences. On the one hand, a democratization of the Sangha is occurring, with various meditative techniques made available to a wider public, which is a positive development. But on the other hand, this path tends to become falsely elitist, because one imitates a monastic tradition that renounces family ties while actually maintaining a householder's life. There is a contradiction here, and how the two will be integrated so that arrogance and hypocrisy will be minimized is still to be seen.

In contrast, while the path of Pure Land is relatively unknown, it is a major form of Buddhism in East Asia. Historically speaking, it was pursued as an adjunct to different schools of Buddhism, until it became an independent school in twelfth-century Japan, in response to the needs of a wide lay following who had been excluded from entering the gates of Buddhism. Shinran carried lay Buddhism a step further and began the tradition of married clergy.

The Shin Buddhist path is the path of my choice, a path that makes no undue demands on its followers, physical or otherwise, except one: *the giving up of the ego-self.* Consistent with the original teaching of Shakyamuni Buddha, Shin regards the ego-self as another human construct but with such deep roots in one's karmic past that it is impossible to give up. Hence, sometimes it is called karmic self, but since it creates suffering for oneself and others, it is also the self of karmic evil. Because of its deep roots in count-less lives past, becoming free of the ego-self so that true and real personhood might emerge is not an easy matter. This is where the working of boundless compassion in the form of the Primal Vow comes to nullify the ego-self and transforms it into its opposite. Since all the work is done by the invisible Other Power, the path of Pure Land is deemed the Easy Path, but to experience this in all its depth and height is another matter. Hence, the scriptures re-mind us that "The path is easy but few are those who take it."[2]

In retrospect, my choice of the path of Pure Land seems to have been inevitable, although it was not that obvious from the beginning. Part of the choice was genetic: I come from several generations of Shin temple families from both of my parents. And part of it was a distaste for authoritarian structures, whether insti-tutional or doctrinal. I find Shinran's way to be the most egalitar-ian among the Buddhist paths, especially knowing that this path was readied for a person like myself—a seeker but a faltering one, always looking for easy answers, yet constantly yearning for recog-nition. Shinran had no disciples and considered all who followed him as fellow seekers, fellow sojourners, and fellow companions (*ondobo, ondogyo*) on the path of enlightenment.

The starting point of the path of Pure Land is the very person standing here and now; and the ultimate conclusion is the grateful awareness that all has been granted us in this very moment. Perhaps it was something like this that led to the following poem by e. e. cummings:

> *Seeker of truth*
> *Follow no path*
> *All paths lead where*
> *Truth is here.*[3]

"Truth is here" tells us that the goal of our spiritual quest is not in transcending our everyday world, or in some far-off place in time and space. It is to be discovered and rediscovered at the very place where we stand. The vision of Pure Land and the image of Amida Buddha are not to be taken literally but figuratively. They aid us in plumbing the depth of our present existence and discovering therein a new order of being, radically refreshing compared to the conventional world built with false constructs. This is also confirmed by T. S. Eliot in the well-known lines from *Little Gidding*:

> *We shall not cease from exploration*
> *And at the end of all our exploring*
> *Will be to arrive where we started*
> *And know the place for the first time.*[4]

"To know the place for the first time" is given a clearer picture and richer content by Alice Walker, the highly acclaimed author of *The Color Purple* and other significant works. In her words:

Heaven. Now there's a thought. Nothing has ever been able, ultimately, to convince me we live anywhere else. And that heaven, more a verb than a noun, more a condition than a place, is all about leading with the heart in whatever broken or ragged state it's in, stumbling forward in faith until, from time to time, we miraculously find our way. Our way to forgiveness, our way of letting go, our way of understanding, compassion and peace. It is laughter, I think, that bubbles up at last and says, "Ho, I think we are there," and that "there" is always here.[5]

The realization of the path of Pure Land, culminating in the here and now, may be said to be reality realizing itself; that is to say, each concrete particular affirmed as manifesting reality-as-it-is is the cornerstone of an interdependent and interconnected world.

A similar awakening is found in a statement by the educator Parker Palmer: "Every 'thing' in the world now possesses the personal name and preciousness of personhood—every rock, every flower, every beast that crawls, every human self. In light of the incarnation the world is no longer an object to be manipulated and owned. Instead, it is a community of persons, and knowing that truth means recovering the bonds of personhood and community that have been lost between us."[6]

Here we must pause and reflect on the meaning of the word "religion" and the need to expand its definition. The word "religion" as we know it did not exist in Asian languages, but when Western civilization was introduced into that part of the world in the modern period, people came up with translations that reflected their own heritage. Searching for a suitable equivalent to translate the term into their vernacular, the Japanese, for example, used the word *shu-kyo* as a translation for "religion." This term is found in Buddhist scriptures; its literal meaning is "the teaching of that which is fundamental." (*Shu* is "fundamental tenet" and *kyo* is "teaching.") It is in this sense that both the path of Sages and path of the Pure Land may be called religion—they teach that which is fundamental for living a meaningful, creative life, including the path or method to that realization.

According to the Pure Land tradition, it was the philosopher Nagarjuna (second and third centuries C.E.), who first characterized the path of Pure Land as the "easy path," in contrast to the path of Sages labeled as the "difficult path." While it is burdensome to carry a heavy load on one's back and travel by foot to reach one's goal, it is much easier to be carried on a ferry and transported on the waterway to the same destination. Thus, the Primal Vow of Amida, the Buddha of Immeasurable Light and Immeasurable Life, is likened to a huge vessel that carries all beings to the other shore of supreme enlightenment. In the words of Shinran,

It is a great torch in the long night of ignorance;
Do not lament that your wisdom-eye is dark.
It is a ship on the vast ocean of birth-and-death;
Do not grieve that your karmic obstructions are heavy.[7]

The Pure Land path may be open to misunderstanding, if and when it is seen through the popular notions of faith-oriented religion. The problem is compounded by another set of well-known Pure Land terms, "self-power" and "Other Power," first enunciated by T'an-luan in the early sixth century. While self-power is identified with the difficult path of Sages and Other Power with the easy path of Pure Land, our concern is with the existence of self-power within Other Power. That is, self-power is the natural inclination to assert the power of the ego-self to reach a goal, but it is necessary to realize that ultimately it is ineffectual and fruitless on the path of supreme enlightenment. Yet, at the same time, it is a necessary stage on the path where self-power is also appreciated, in reflection, as the working of Other Power.

The proper relationship of these two terms may be illustrated by the example of sailing on the high seas. In order for the sailboat to catch the wind (Other Power), the sailor must first undertake a variety of tasks (self-power). The sails, of course, must be put up, but countless unseen preparations are necessary: studying the weather forecasts, judging the prevailing wind velocity and the movements of the ocean currents, mastering the use of various navigational tools—the sextant, charts, dividers, current tables, tide tables, depth finder, radar, VHF radio, and so on. All this requires time, effort, and hard work, similar to the preliminary work required on the Pure Land path.

All this preparation, however, will not move the ship. When all preparations have been completed and the sails have been hoisted, one must now wait with patience and alertness for the wind to blow. Such a state of waiting is required, for the wind of

Other Power is beyond human control. When the wind does blow, however, the sailboat is ready to cruise effortlessly on the high seas with lightness and alacrity.

Such must have been the feeling of Shinran, who, after twenty years of relentless quest and search as a Tendai monk, abandoned it for the path of nembutsu. His joy is expressed with exuberance:

> Now, as I ride on the ship of the great compassionate vow and sail on the expansive ocean of wondrous light, the breeze of highest virtue blows peacefully and calms the waves of pain and sorrow. Quickly shall I reach the land of immeasurable light and attain unexcelled peace and freedom.[8]

When freed from egoistic designs and calculations, life unfolds freely, in spite of unavoidable difficulties. But a new kind of wisdom is bestowed on a person, so that he or she can negotiate through the labyrinth called life.

Wisdom, however, is not something acquired or gained, as in the Path of Sages; rather, it is bestowed or granted to the person of nembutsu who is a foolish being. According to Shinran,

> When a person accepts and entrusts the self to the Name of the Buddha of Inconceivable wisdom-light, holding it in mindfulness, Avalokitesvara and Mahasthamaprapta accompany the person constantly, as shadows do things. . . . A sutra states that Avalokitesvara, with the name of Bodhisattva Treasure-response, reveals himself as the god of the sun and dispels the pitch darkness of ignorance of all beings; and Mahasthamaprapta, with the name of Bodhisattva Treasure-happiness, reveals himself as the god of the moon and illuminates the long night of birth-and-death. Together they bring forth wisdom in all beings.[9]

Thus, Shinran concludes, "To entrust oneself to the nembutsu is to already have become a person who realizes wisdom and will attain Buddhahood; know that this is to become free of foolishness. Hence the expression, 'The Buddha of the light of wisdom' is used."[10]

樹心弘誓佛地

流念難思法海

釋華書

PART TWO

Unfolding Awareness

11

A Wasted Life

The awareness of timeless time, the eternal now, in this present moment is born from an experience, whereby our everyday life becomes the object of doubt and questioning. Death and dying may ultimately awaken us to the fragility of human existence, but it may then be too late. Questions, however, regarding the meaning of our existence may dawn upon us at any time in different benign forms. What we once deeply cherished and held in high regard, for example, may turn out to be hollow and meaningless.

We find this realization frequently among highly accomplished athletes who experience unforseen tragedies, forcing them to shift their priorities. In the basketball season of 2000–2001, this happened to the NBA superstar Alonzo Mourning of the Miami Heat, who was diagnosed with kidney problems and suddenly had to forget about playing basketball; or Marcus Camby of the New York Knicks, whose sisters and mother were kept hostage while the police negotiated their release, preventing him from becoming fully involved in the season-ending tournaments. For both, basketball was their way of life until they suddenly realized that there are more important things to live for. As John Lennon reminded us, Life is what happens when you're busy making other plans.

We all experience such unexpected happenings, and when they hit us, it is a sign that something is making us question the meaning and purpose of our life. There is nothing more tragic than a wasted life. Since this is the only human life we will ever have in eternity, it is incumbent upon us to make it truly real and significant.

A recent Japanese film, entitled "After Life," explores the question of the meaning of life in a subtle, entertaining way. The movie revolves around an unusual plot—people who have died must pass through a drab office staffed by caseworkers who ask each person to recall the most memorable event in his or her life. They are given three days to come up with an answer. Once a person remembers something unforgettable, the staff makes a videotape to approximate the event. Each person receives a copy that he or she takes to the next world.

The office workers are actually all dead people who failed to recall anything memorable, and so they could not pass into the next world. They are serving time in this office, which is a transit station between this life and the next, although this is never fully explained in the film. It is interesting to note that the literal translation of the Japanese title of the film, "Wonderful Life," was changed for the American audience to "After Life." This gives a sharper focus to the main thrust of the film: What is it that makes one's life worthwhile, the memory of which one can take to the next life?

Various events are recounted by the people passing through the office. One gentleman remembers flying solo for the first time, an elderly man brags about his amorous conquests (which turn out to be false), an old woman recalls from her childhood a lovely picnic under colorful cherry blossoms, a defiant young man refuses to make any choice. A little girl mentions Disneyland, but thirty others have already chosen it, so she must find another memory.

One seventy-two-year-old gentleman can't recall anything from his life, so he must spend time viewing seventy-two videotapes, one for each year, trying to recall some special event in his life. His marriage had been arranged, and for him it was nothing but drudgery. He seeks desperately to find something that gave him happiness in life. When the office worker in charge of this gentleman watched the videos with him, to his surprise he notices that the man's wife was once his own lover. When he suddenly died as a young man of twenty, his girlfriend was left all alone, but evidently she got married to this gentleman. Reminded of this short but happy romance in his youth, the office worker recalls it fondly and passes his test, so that he can leave the drab office and move on to the next world.

After the movie, I asked myself, if I had to pass through such a process after my death, what would I claim as the most memorable event in my life? What would I choose, so that I could move on to the next world? Could I come up with something truly significant that might prompt me to say, "Yes, my life was a good life, a memorable life?" Or might I have to admit to a boring life and confess, "I have wasted my life"?

Friedrich Nietzsche foresaw the onslaught of nihilism in nineteenth-century European life. His warning cry, "The wasteland grows; woe to him who hides wastelands within!" still echoes today. The increasing violence in our society is evidence of the emptiness and aimlessness at the core of contemporary life world-wide. T. S. Eliot heeded this warning and captured it in his famous critique of civilization, *The Waste Land*. Although it appeared in 1922, it is still relevant for our times, and the concluding yearning for peace, repeated in Sanskrit, still remains— *"shantih, shantih, shantih."*[1]

1 2

Self-Delusion

According to the Chinese transmission of the Vinaya, the Buddha set out alone to Uruvela, after dispatching fifty disciples to spread the Buddha Dharma to various parts of the country.[1] On the way he rested in a grove and sat in meditation under a tree. It so happened that thirty couples were on a picnic nearby; all were married couples, except for one young bachelor who brought along a woman from the demimonde. While everyone was enjoying the picnic, they suddenly noticed that this woman was missing.

When they looked around for her, they discovered that she had disappeared with all their valuables.

They began a frantic search for her throughout the picnic grounds and the nearby woods, whereupon they came upon the Buddha seated in meditation. Seeing the young people running around, the Buddha asked what they were doing. When they told him that they were looking for the woman who disappeared with their belongings, he said, "Which is more important—searching for the woman or seeking your true self?" The Buddha convinced them of the importance of self-knowledge, and they all immediately became his disciples.

Our search for the objects of happiness—love, material success, wealth, good position, recognition, and honor—is normally outside of ourselves. Rare is the person who turns inward to come to know all the hidden dimensions of himself or herself. But this is important, because we can live without knowing everything about the world, especially in our increasingly complex age, but we cannot be fully alive without knowing ourselves. Awakening to the true self has been the central quest in the Buddhist life, succinctly stated in the classic statement by the Zen master Dogen (1200–1253):

> *To study the Buddha Dharma is*
> *to study the self.*
> *To study the self is*
> *to forget the self.*
> *To forget the self is*
> *to be confirmed by ten thousand things.*[2]

The focus here is on forgetting the delusory self; we think we know ourselves, when in fact the darkness of ignorance enfolds us and we fail to see the self. Thus, the first step in pursuing the Buddha Dharma is to become freed from the false, delusory self and to let the true self be "confirmed by the ten thousand things."

Reality affirms all things, including the self, just as they are. This affirmation of phenomenal particulars has been expressed variously since early in Buddhism as the realization of suchness (*tathata*), thatness (*tattva*), or thingness (*dharmata*).

As noted earlier, Pure Land Buddhism speaks of two paths to self-knowledge—the path of Sages, referring to the monastics, and the path of Pure Land for the laity. While their goals are one and the same, their approaches are different. This was clearly expressed by Honen, who said: "In the path of Sages, one perfects wisdom and attains enlightenment; in the path of Pure Land, one returns to the foolish self to be saved by Amida."[3]

Everyone is subject to self-delusion. Teachers of the Buddha Dharma are especially prone to this delusion, because their status requires them to be wiser and more understanding than their students. But, no matter how wise they may appear, they are still human and cannot control powerful instinctual forces: the need for attention and praise, occasional eruptions of anger, awakening of repressed sexuality, countless questions posed to them that have no answers. Shinran's admission, when he compared himself to his teacher Honen, is instructive:

The true entrusting of the wise is such that they are inwardly wise but outwardly foolish.

The heart of this ignorant one is such that I am inwardly foolish but outwardly wise.[4]

The "wise" in the initial statement refers to his teacher Honen, who may present himself to the public as being foolish but, in fact, is truly wise. This is the opposite with Shinran, "this ignorant one," who shows himself off as the wise but keeps foolishness hidden within.

On the Shin Buddhist path one is made to recognize self-delusion, having been once illuminated by the light of boundless compassion. This recognition continues throughout one's lifetime, but we are also shown that the delusions are never permanent, for the light of compassion ultimately begins the process of transformation, so that delusions become transmuted into sources of wisdom, making a person more true, real, and sincere.

We see this process of change dramatically illustrated in the career of the "whiskey priest" who is the unnamed protagonist in Graham Greene's novel *The Power and the Glory*. The narrative centers on a manhunt for a Catholic priest escaping the law in the jungles and mountains of Mexico. He is the last priest in the state where religion has been outlawed. The gradual downfall of the priest begins initially with a description of smug piety, sanctity, and holiness and culminates in a jail cell, where he sees himself as he truly is—broken, sinful, and unworthy even of hell. He goes to God empty, unable to forswear whiskey, incapable of renouncing lust, condemned by parishioners. But having been stripped of the externals of religious authority, admitting doubt and failure, he is now closer to God than at any previous moment in his life: "He felt only an immense disappointment because he had to go to God empty-handed, with nothing done at all."[5] But that ultimately is his salvation: "Where sin increased, grace abounded all the more" (Rom. 5:20).

This novel is said to have been originally titled *Labyrinthine Ways,* based on the poem "The Hound of Heaven" by Francis Thompson:

> *I fled Him, down the nights and down the days;*
> *I fled Him, down the arches of the years;*
> *I fled Him, down the labyrinthine ways*
> *   of my own mind; and in the mist of tears*
> *I hid from Him, and under running laughter.*
> *   Up vistaed hopes I sped; and shot, precipitated*
> *Adown titanic glooms of chasmed fears*
> *From those strong Feet that followed, followed after.*[6]

We find a similar phenomenon in Shinran, who explains the Japanese term for "grasp" (*sesshu*) as the primary function of boundless compassion. The word consists of two parts, *setsu* plus *shu*. *Setsu* means to pursue and grasp the one who seeks to run away, and *shu* means to receive and embrace. According to Shinran:

> *Seeing the sentient beings of the nembutsu*
> *Throughout the worlds, countless as particles, in the ten quarters,*
> *The Buddha grasps and never abandons them,*
> *And therefore is named "Amida."*[7]

13

Subliminal Self

Shinran speaks of true entrusting as twofold: entrusting oneself to the finite, limited karmic reality that is this foolish, *bonbu* self, and simultaneously entrusting oneself to boundless and immeasurable compassion that enfolds it. The latter is the working of dharma (rendered as *ho* in Japanese) and the former is the spiritual potential fully realized (denoted as *ki*). The unity of the two is the crux of Shin religious life, called *ki-ho ittai* (*ittai* means "unity").

This unity of *ki* and *ho* is basic to Pure Land tradition, summed up as follows:

> Deep mind is the deeply entrusting mind. There are two aspects. First is to believe deeply and decidedly that one is a foolish being of karmic evil caught in birth-and-death, ever sinking and ever wandering in transmigration from innumerable kalpas in the past with never a condition that would lead to emancipation. Second is to believe deeply and decidedly that Amida Buddha's Forty-eight Vows grasp sentient beings, and that allowing oneself to be carried by the power of the Vow without any doubt or apprehension, one will attain birth.[1]

Both are essential for a holistic self-realization—the unity of *ki* and *ho*, integration of light and darkness, harmonizing of conscious and unconscious, the simultaneous descent downward of instinctual passions and the flight upward into transcendence.[2]

The subliminal self is deeply rooted in our karmic past, beyond any human comprehension. This is clarified in the Yogachara school of Buddhism, which analyzes human consciousness into eight *vijnanas*, sometimes rendered as "consciousness." They include the five senses plus the sixth, which is ordinary consciousness, the seventh, which is the subliminal self-centered consciousness, called *manas*, and the eighth, which is the storehouse consciousness, *alaya-vijnana*, understood as the ground of life itself. The subliminal self, beyond ordinary detection and control, governs our conscious life.

While Shin Buddhism normally does not refer to Yogachara philosophy, implicit in its teaching is the vast and profound tradition of *samadhi* which gave shape and form to this analysis of human consciousness, including the transformation thereof. When Shinran speaks of karmic evil and blind passions, he makes explicit in ordinary language the insight into the seventh consciousness or subliminal self, *manas,* at the core of our being.

I once taught a seminar on comparative meditative practices at my college. On the final day of the course, I invited a friend who was a pioneer in biofeedback research to conduct a workshop for my students. Since he also practiced Zen meditation, I wanted him to explain the differences and similarities between biofeedback and Zen. As part of the workshop, each student experimented with the simple biofeedback equipment my friend brought to class. They tested muscle tension, blood pressure, and brain waves. Everyone was deeply engrossed in their experiments, when suddenly one student said, "Mr. Unno, you should try one." I demurred, saying, "We don't have enough machines, and besides I don't think we have enough time left." But my friend pulled out a simple clip-on metal gadget, and he put it on my fingertip. Attached to it was an electric wire connected to a little box that gave off sound.

The moment the clip was put on my finger, it gave off a buzzing, fluctuating sound. So I said, "Give me ten seconds." I closed my eyes, relaxed my shoulders, dropped the tensions in my body to the pit of my stomach, and focused on my *ki,* or *ch'i.* Immediately silence prevailed, and the fluctuating buzzing stopped and turned into a slow and even sound. Several seconds passed. Then I heard a whisper coming from the corner of the room, "Geez, he's pretty good!" That instant, the buzzing sound started again; this time loudly, "BzzzzBZZZZ, bzzzBZZZZ, bzzzz-BZZZbzzz." No matter how hard I tried, I could not control or stop the fluctuating sound. My subconscious had been rattled by a few words of praise, and there was nothing that I could do to control it.

This simple episode reminded me again that I live on two levels—the surface, conscious level and the subliminal level, beyond my recognition or control. To achieve wholeness we need to become aware of this subliminal self, not through some kind of therapy or analysis—which is a conscious function, after all—but through the illumination that not only brings to awareness the self-delusion at the core of our being but also transmutes it into an open, positive, life-giving energy. Whether we are aware or not, the light of boundless compassion constantly illuminates our total being.

14

Symbolism of Light

Among religious symbols, light is one of the most common and pervasive, and its corollary, darkness, is equally universal. The relationship between the two is complex and varies with traditions. At one extreme we have, for example, the Chinese symbol of *yin* and *yang,* showing that darkness and light are interpenetrating and complimentary, essential for cosmic creativity. On the other hand, we have in Zoroastrianism the combat between light and darkness, Ahura Mazda and Angra Mainyu. The bipolar relationship of light and darkness in Christianity is also well known: the power of God in conflict with Satan, the Prince of Evil and Darkness. Our purpose here, however, is to simply identify the countless references to light in world religions, which will provide a context for clarifying the significance of light in the Pure Land tradition.

In the monotheistic tradition, light is identified with the Supreme Being. In the Hebrew Bible we find countless references, such as "The lord is my light and salvation" (Ps. 27:1). According to Isaiah 60:19,

> *The sun shall be no more*
> *your light by day,*
> *nor for brightness shall the moon*
> *give light to you by night;*
> *but the Lord will be your everlasting light.*

The indwelling of God in man, *shekhinah,* is called the "created splendor of light."

The New Testament references to Jesus inherit this imagery: "In him was life, and the life was the light of men. The light shines in the darkness, and the darkness has not overcome it" (John 1:4–5); and "I am the light of the world; he who follows me will not walk in darkness, but will have the light of life" (John 8:12). My favorite passage from the Gospel of John reads:

> The light is with you for a little longer. Walk while you have the light, lest the darkness overtakes you; he who walks in the darkness does not know where he goes. While you have the light, believe in the light, that you become sons of light (John 12:35–36).

We find a similar assertion in Islam concerning Allah, the source of light as proclaimed in the *Koran*:

Allah is the light of the heavens and the earth. His light may be compared to a niche that enshrines a lamp, the lamp within a crystal of star-like brilliance. It is lit from the blessed olive tree neither eastern nor western. Its very oil would almost shine forth, though no fire touch it. Light upon light; Allah guides to his light whom He will.[1]

It is no wonder that the symbolism of light also plays a central role among Sufi mystics. Light was given an intellectual and ethical nuance in Greek philosophy, which influenced both Christianity and Islam.

When we turn to ancient India, with its rich naturalistic polytheism, one of the supreme gods is Surya:

> *Athwart the darkness gazing up.*
> *To him the higher light, we*
> *Have soared to Surya, the god*
> *Among the gods, the highest light.*[2]

The Hindu classic *Brihadaranyaka-Upanishad* (IV.3.6) relates the story of King Janaka, who asks his teacher, Yajnavalkya, about the light by which man is guided. The teacher gives a series of answers—light of sun, moon, fire, speech—and then this exchange occurs:

> When the sun has set, Yajnavalkya, and the moon has set, and the fire has gone out and speech has stopped, what light does a person have? "The self (*atman*), indeed, is his light," said he, "for with the self, indeed, as the light, one sits, moves about, does one's work and returns."[3]

The self (*atman*) as the personal divine center is light which unites with Brahman, the cosmic divine center. The unbounded joy of being bathed in light is celebrated by Rabindranath Tagore (1861–1941), the Nobel Prize recipient for literature:

> Light, my light, the world-filling light, the eye-kissing light, heart-sweetening light!
> Ah, the light dances, my darling, at the centre of my life; the light strikes, my darling, the chords of my love; the sky opens, the wind runs wild, laughter passes over the earth.
> The butterflies spread their sails on the sea of light. Lilies and jasmines surge up on the crest of the waves of light.
> The light is shattered into gold on every cloud, my darling, and it scatters gems in profusion.[4]

In Chinese meditative practice, light is identified with the *ch'i*-energy, as found in the Taoist classic *Secret of the Golden Flower*. The integration of self is achieved through the circulation of light:

> The light is neither inside nor outside the self. Mountains, rivers, sun, moon, and the whole earth are all this light, so it is not only in the self. All the operation of intelligence, knowledge, and wisdom are also this light, so it is not outside the self. The light of heaven and earth fills the universe; the light of one individual also naturally extends through the heavens and covers the earth.
>
> Therefore once you turn the light around, everything in the world is turned around.[5]

We now turn to the implications of light in Pure Land Buddhism. First, light is identified with Amida Buddha, as is evident in the original Sanskrit, *amitabha* or "Immeasurable Light." Second, light is symbolic of wisdom, since the illumination by Immeasurable Light endows us with the ability to see delusions, both within and without. The principal characteristic of Immeasurable Light is that it takes in foolish beings of blind passion without judgment or hesitation and transforms them into awakened beings endowed with wisdom. These qualities are experienced internally, but they cannot be known objectively.

That light is an internal realization is pointed out by Jacques Lusseyran, the French Resistance leader. He lost his sight in both eyes at the age of seven, when he was shoved from behind and his face struck the corner of a school table. But he made up for his blindness as he grew up by developing a heightened sensitivity in his other faculties, enabling him to successfully overcome life's many challenges to become a leader in the French Resistance during World War II. At the end of his autobiography, *And There Was Light,* he leaves two legacies:

> The first of these is that joy does not come from outside, for whatever happens to us, it is within. The second is that light does not come from without. Light is within us, even if we have no eyes to see.[6]

Our tendency is to look for the source of happiness outside of ourselves, whether it be love, material acquisitions, or worldly recognition, when in fact it can come only from deep within ourselves. We also mistakenly believe that the light that illuminates our existence and brings us self-knowledge comes from the outside, but it, too, comes from within ourselves. Although sightless, Lusseyran sees both truths with acute insight and clarity.

That light cannot be known directly is expressed in contemporary terms by Peter Russell. When speaking of the light of consciousness, he asserts:

> Although all we ever see is light, paradoxically, we never know light directly. The light that strikes the eye is known

only through the energy it releases. This energy is translated into a visual imagery in the mind, and that image seems to be composed of light—but that light is a quality of mind. We never know the light itself.[7]

Russell is speaking from a scientific viewpoint, but the fact that we can never know light itself is helpful in appreciating the working of boundless compassion. When the light of compassion illuminates our existence, it reveals our self-delusions. Hiroyuki Itsuki, the noted author of *Tariki: Embracing Despair, Discovering Peace,* describes this as follows:

> We cannot know that we are illuminated by a great light simply by looking up into the sky. But if we lower our heads and look down at our feet we can clearly see the long, dark shadow that stretches out from us. We know that the darker and blacker that shadow is, the brighter the light that shines upon us.[8]

The abundance of light manifested by Amida Buddha comes through clearly in his twelve names, all capturing the multifaceted working of light. Amida is also called the Buddha of Immeasurable Light, Buddha of Unhindered Light, Buddha of Immaculate Light, Buddha of Joyful Light, Buddha of Wisdom Light, Buddha of Incomparable Light, Buddha of Majestic Light, Buddha of Unceasing Light, Buddha of Light More Luminous than Sun and Moon, Buddha of Improbable Light, Buddha of Indescribable Light, and Buddha of Inconceivable Light.[9] It should be underscored that we are not talking about some supernatural being emanating rays of light in all directions. Rather, when our life becomes illuminated by the light of compassion, simultaneously enriched by deep hearing of the Buddha Dharma, we awaken to light that makes us see things, including the self, as they are.

According to Shinran in his *Hymns of the Pure Land,* there are three virtues of light to be praised. First is its all-embracing quality that illumines and awakens each sentient being:

> *The light of wisdom exceeds all measure,*
> *And every finite being*
> *Receives this illumination that is like the dawn,*
> *So take refuge in Amida, the true and real light.*[10]

Second is its illumination of our delusions that are dispelled from the three courses of existence—life in hell, life as hungry spirits, and life as animals:

> *The Buddha's light is supreme in radiance;*
> *Thus Amida is called "Buddha, Lord of Blazing Light."*
> *It dispels the darkness of the three courses of affliction,*
> *So take refuge in Amida, the Great One worthy of offerings.*[11]

Ultimately, light is celebrated as the source of transformation that enables us to relish the joy of dharma:

> *The light of compassion illumines us from afar;*
> *Those beings it reaches, it is taught,*
> *Attain the joy of dharma,*
> *So take refuge in Amida, the great consolation.*[12]

In brief, the salutary effect of light is summed up in Pure Land scripture with the words: "When living beings come into contact with this light, the three kinds of defilements disappear in them. Their bodies and minds become supple and gentle. They become full of joy and enthusiasm and good thoughts arise in them."[13]

The main function of light is to transform the darkness of ignorance, blind passion, and karmic evil into their very opposites, making them essential components of enlightenment. Thus, Shinran sings,

> *Through the benefit of unhindered light,*
> *We realize shinjin of vast, majestic virtues,*
> *And the ice of our blind passions necessarily melts,*
> *Immediately becoming the water of enlightenment.*[14]

The ultimate end of this transformation is nothing less than supreme enlightenment itself:

> *The unhindered light filling the ten quarters*
> *Shines on the beings in the darkness of ignorance*
> *And unfailingly brings to attainment of nirvana*
> *The person who realizes the one thought-moment of joy.*[15]

Although Shinran preferred Immeasurable Light (*amitabha*) when referring to Amida, especially in his later years, light is inseparable from life (*amitayus*). The intimate connection between light and life may be seen in the following story that I once heard from a person who struggled to understand the working of the boundless light of compassion.

He was deeply tormented for years, because no matter how hard he tried, he could not make sense of the significance of Immeasurable Light in his own life. One day he read of a man who worked in one of the famous limestone caves in Japan. This man reported that before the caves were discovered by tourists, the exploration in the underground darkness was treacherous and dangerous. Since one could not see in the pitch-black darkness, one could easily sprain an ankle, break a leg, or even fall off a ledge and hurt oneself badly. To make it safer for tourists, the local authorities brought in electricity and installed lightbulbs throughout the long cave.

Soon after the lightbulbs began illuminating the darkness, the

man noticed something he had never seen before—mosses growing here and there. Nothing had grown in the darkness of the
cave, but when electricity was brought in, the mosses grew in response to the light. My friend suddenly realized a simple and obvious truth—without light there is no life, but with light new life
is born and grows, even in the darkest of places.

Although at times we may feel that we live only in darkness,
we are constantly reminded that the light of compassion shines
upon us without ceasing, illuminating our existence. In the words
of Shinran,

> *Although my eyes filled with blind passion*
> *Cannot see the light that embraces me,*
> *Great Compassion ceaselessly*
> *Illuminates my darkness.*[16]

When we are awakened to the efflorescence of light, the interdependent and interconnected nature of reality also becomes
real. This fact is expressed metaphorically by the interpenetration
of light emanating from the flowers blooming in the realm of enlightened beings:

Each jewel blossom has a hundred thousand million petals.
The radiant light emanating from their petals is of countless
different colors. . . . The splendor of each ray of each of
these lights surpasses the radiance of the sun and the moon.
From every flower issue thirty-six hundred thousand million
rays of light. From each of these rays issue thirty-six hundred
thousand million buddhas. . . . Moreover, each one of those
buddhas emits hundreds of thousands of rays of light that
spread out everywhere in the ten quarters and proclaim the
subtle and sublime Dharma. In this way, each of these buddhas firmly establishes innumerable living beings in the
Buddha's True Way.[17]

15

Compassion that Nurtures

Among the countless Buddhas that are found in the Mahayana universe, including Akshobhya Buddha, Maitreya Buddha, Vairochana Buddha, Medicine Buddha, and so on, Amida Buddha stands out as the Great Compassionate One, nurturing the spirituality of all beings without discrimination. This is the reason that Amida is called *Oya-sama* in vernacular Japanese. *Oya* means "close, intimate, nurturing," and refers to one's parent, whether mother or father; *sama* is an honorific. The term suggests a loving parent who is always encouraging, supporting, and nurturing a child, especially a weak and fragile child.

While this compassionate nature of the Buddha of Immeasurable Light and Life originates from the heart of Mahayana Buddhism, it undergoes further development in Japan, where receptivity to the maternal further enhanced the compassionate aspect of Amida. The function of the maternal principle is to embrace everyone, good or bad, discounting merits or demerits, and treating a person as if he or she were one's only child. In the words of Shinran,

> *The Tathagata of Light that Surpasses the Sun and Moon*
> *Taught me the nembutsu-samadhi.*
> *The Tathagatas of the ten quarters compassionately regard*
> *Each sentient being as their only child.*[1]

Since the middle of the nineteenth century, foreign Christian missionaries have invested time, money, and energy into spreading the gospel in Japan. But Japanese Christians number less than one percent of the total population, even though the Christian impact on the intellectual and cultural life of Japan has been immense. The lack of success in the missionary field is ascribed to many factors, one of the primary ones being the patriarchal image of the Western monotheistic God.

Archbishop Leo Ikenaga of Osaka made this point when he said, "One reason for the small number of conversions in Asia is that Western Christianity has been preaching too masculine a God and emphasizing the division between God and the universe. The Asian Church needs to stress the more 'maternal traits' of God."[2] A similar sentiment is expressed by Father Yoji Inouye:

> For me Christ is not a patriarchal God, but a God who especially embraces and feels sorry for a weak, spoiled child. Jesus' prayer always begins with "Abba!" It is something a

child held in a parent's arms says to a loving father: it is not a word directed to a God of anger and judgement.[3]

The problem of a patriarchal God in relation to feminism and ecological consciousness is dealt with in a highly sophisticated manner by Aloysius Pieris in a series of works, the most recent being *Fire and Water: Basic Issues in Asian Buddhism and Christianity.*[4]

The questioning of the traditional image of God is also a major theme in the works of the Japanese Catholic novelist Shusaku Endo. In one of his essays, he discusses the nature of religion as he understands it:

To me there are two kinds of religion. Erich Fromm called them father-religion and mother-religion. In father-religion, God is to be feared; he judges and punishes man's sins: he gets angry. Mother-religion is different. God is to man what a mother is to a bad child. God forgives; God suffers with man. As it is written in the *Tannisho,* if the righteous are saved, how much more so the wicked.[5]

The *Tannisho,* or *Lamenting the Deviations,* is a Shin Buddhist tract containing the sayings of Shinran that were compiled by his disciple several decades after the master's death.[6] Endo goes on to reflect on the state of Christianity in Japan:

I began to feel that the gulf I had long felt between Christianity and me was due to European overemphasis on the paternal aspect of religion. Christianity seemed distant to us Japanese because the other aspect, maternal religion, had been grossly neglected from the time of the early Christian missionaries down to the present.[7]

Among Endo's many novels, perhaps the best known is *Silence,* a narrative set in the late sixteenth century in Kyushu, when

Christianity is proscribed by the Tokugawa government primarily for political reasons, a major one being the fear of the encroachment of Western imperialism, spearheaded by Portugal and Spain, into East Asia.

The banning of Christianity and the persecution of Japanese Christians took various forms, ranging from forced renunciation of faith to execution for resisting apostasy. One of the standard tests required was stepping on the *fumi-e,* a copper plate with the crucifix engraved upon it. Trampling on the face of Jesus meant the repudiation of one's Christian faith. The men and women of strong faith refused to recant, and many were executed and later celebrated as martyrs. The strong-willed Portuguese Jesuit Sebastian Rodrigues in the beginning condemned the weak Christians who had apostasized, but in the end he himself relented, when he heard the sympathetic voice of Jesus Christ:

> *Trample! Trample! I more than anyone know of the pain in your foot.*
> *Trample! It was to be trampled on by men that I was born into this world.*
> *It was to share men's pain that I carried my cross.*[8]

In brief, God's mercy identifies with the weak, powerless, and exhausted, not the strong of faith who die a glorious martyrdom. The maternal Jesus forgives the sin of apostasy. Thus, Endo concludes his novel: "It was not a Christ whose face was filled with majesty and glory; neither was it a face made beautiful by endurance of pain; nor was it a face filled with the strength of will that has repelled temptation. The face of the man who then lay at his feet was sunken and utterly exhausted."[9] Although Endo is criticized by New Testament scholars,[10] his emphasis on the maternal seems significant today, especially when people hunger for tenderness, love, and compassion.

Although the persecution of Christians in Japan is well known, an even greater persecution of Shin Buddhists occurred in various parts of Japan beginning in the late sixteenth century for primarily political reasons. The persecution was harshest in the present-day prefectures of Kagoshima, Miyazaki, and Kumamoto in southern Kyushu, and it did not end until 1877, when the law banning Shin Buddhism was repealed.

During this period of almost three hundred years, Shin Buddhists went underground, meeting secretly to avoid detection by the authorities, and held their religious services in hidden caves, remote forests, and offshore boats. When they were caught, they were tortured, made to confess their illegal activities, and executed when they refused to divulge the names of fellow believers. But apostasy seems not to have been such a critical issue. It may be due to the all-embracing and nonjudgmental compassion of Amida, whose commitment is the salvation of the weak, ignorant, and lost. This is evident in the closing remark of a Shin faithful in a video documentary on the persecuted Shin Buddhists of Kagoshima: "I can discard the nembutsu, if I'm told to, but Amida-sama will never abandon me."[11]

The welcoming arms of Amida, who receives everyone without discrimination or judgment, is expressed by Jutaro Oshima, one of the early Japanese immigrants to Hawaii:

> *Although the voice that calls*
> NAMU–AMIDA–BUTSU *is mine,*
> *It is the voice of Oya-sama calling me,*
> *"Come as you are!"*[12]

The returning home to the bosom of boundless compassion was expressed in an intimate, personal way by my good friend George Foot, founder and president of Newgate LLP. A voracious reader and once-aspiring writer, he had reread my book *River of*

Fire, River of Water several times and even wrote a book review to post on Amazon, but it was rejected. He was told that it was too personal.[13] But George wanted me to have a copy of the review which he sent me with a cover letter that read:

> Your wonderful book, a gift in so many ways, was such a delight that I could not write you until I read it several times. Marooned somewhere between Dionysian Greece and Walden Pond, your romancing, singing, weaving of the Pure Land faith spoke deeply to me. As an adolescent I would frequently escape the burden of house and family and walk, often in deep winter, to a nearby park. There I'd shin my way up a friendly apple tree and watch the painfully brilliant stars rotate above me. Knowing nothing, understanding nothing, overwhelmed by the sheer beauty and grace of life. Then, with numbed fingers and toes, I'd trudge back to a lower-class life that I loathed. Yet, every time as I reached the crest of the hill and looked down at my parent's house, I always felt an inexplicable warmth and gratitude that I never fully understood. Now I know that the stars, the cold night air, the porch light my mother always left on for me, conspired to awaken in me a compassion that whispered, "Yes, come home, come just as you are."[14]

George loved visiting Greece and wandering around Walden Pond. And the last quotation is the beckoning call of boundless compassion, reaching us through the Name-that-calls, NAMU-AMIDA-BUTSU.

Regardless of who we are, we are all recipients of the working of boundless compassion, "the ultimate benefit of being grasped never to be abandoned."[15] So it was that George responded to the call "Come home, come just as you are" on August 17, 2000, when he passed away at the vigorous age of fifty-four due to brain tumor. During his final moments, he was surrounded by his loved ones, who chanted "NAMU-AMIDA-BUTSU" continuously for an hour and a half, as he quietly departed for the Home of homes. His cremated ashes rest at his beloved Epidavros, Greece, and at Sharon Gardens in Valhalla, New York, but he lives whenever and wherever the Name-that-calls is intoned.

16

Living the
Buddha Dharma

Japanese immigrants came to Hawaii and the west coast of the mainland U.S. beginning in the late nineteenth and early twentieth centuries. They came as replacements for the Chinese laborers, who were banned by the Chinese Exclusion Act of 1887. Like their Chinese predecessors, the Japanese suffered discrimination and racism of every conceivable kind, both local and national. Japanese immigration was banned in 1907 by executive decree, and all immigration from East Asia finally ended in 1924 by the enactment of the Asian Exclusion Law. Discrimination against the Japanese in the U.S. continued and culminated in 1942 with the mass evacuation and incarceration of 120,000 Japanese Americans, 77,000 of whom were American citizens by birth. This shameful act in American history, carried out without due process of law, was aptly called "the legalization of racism" by the then U.S. Supreme Court Justice Frank Murphy.

The majority of Japanese immigrants came from prefectures that were the strongholds of Shin Buddhism—Hiroshima, Yamaguchi, Wakayama, Fukuoka, and Kumamoto. These prefectures were relatively well-to-do compared to the poorer ones in the northern parts of Japan. Shin Buddhists defied government orders for infanticide during times of drought, their crime rate was always lower than the national average, and most were also fairly well educated for their time. Inheriting a strong Shin faith that sustained them as they struggled to survive in an alien, hostile land, they built Buddhist temples as their community centers.

One of the unique Japanese American communities in Hawaii was located in Kona on the Big Island. They were the pioneers who produced the world-famous Kona coffee by cultivating the well-drained basaltic soil on the hillside, a twenty-mile stretch of land near the ocean. It became world famous when Mark Twain remarked, "I think that Kona coffee has a richer flavor than any other; be it grown where it may and call it by what name you please."[1]

Kona also produced a number of devout Shin Buddhists considered to be *myokonin,* exemplary nembutsu practitioners. In spite of the harsh conditions, demanding labor under relentless sun, minimal pay, and meager subsistence, their nembutsu faith flourished and sustained them. A remarkable collection of poems written in free verse is contained in a slim volume entitled *Dharma Treasures: Spiritual Insights from Hawaii's Shin Buddhist Pioneers,* edited by Tatsuo Muneto.

One fine example of Shin faith in this book is expressed by

Iwaichi Nakamura. He lived to a ripe old age and reminisces about his past:

> *Looking back on the journey of my eighty years,*
> *tightly bound by the rope of blind desire and karmic evil,*
> *I was unable to be free, put into a straight jacket.*
>
> *But, now having the rope of my karmic evil and hindrances cut off*
>   *by the sword of Amida's wisdom,*
> *there are no clouds covering my heart.*
> *What a joy, saying* NAMU–AMIDA–BUTSU
> *in a bright, clear world!*[2]

Nakamura likens the awakening of shinjin to a sword that cuts off the consequences of karmic evil. The metaphor "the sword of Amida's wisdom" was first used by Shan-tao, the Chinese Pure Land master, who wrote, "Like a keen sword is the Name of Amida. With one recitation all evil is removed."[3] Taira Sato, director of a Shin institution in London called Three Wheels, quotes the myokonin Saichi, who also speaks of the sword of Amida:

> *The Name of the Parent cuts too well,*
>   *Too sharp to feel is the Parent's Name.*
> *Not conscious of the borderline between "Namu"*
>   *and "Amida Butsu"—*
> *Such is the sharpness of the six-syllable Name.*
>
> *Self and Other Power are one, through the kindness*
>   *and compassion of the Parent.*
> *To this does Saichi surrender.*[4]

Amida is frequently referred to as "parent" (*oya*), suggesting a close, intimate relationship, and "six-syllable Name" refers to the

Name of Amida, *na-mu-a-mi-da-bu(tsu)*. Sato gives his interpretation of the sword metaphor:

> In this act, what has actually been cut is the discriminating intellect which stood between "Namu" and "Amida Butsu" trying somehow to force them together. The keen edge of the Name has cut off the attachments of the rationalizing mind to its own self-power. With this severed, "Namu" is just "Namu" and "Amida Butsu" is just "Amida Butsu," and herein lies the realization of the absolute "Namu Amida Butsu" where both self (Namu) and Other Power (Amida Butsu) are one, and at the same time both independent and just as they are.[5]

Nakamura also speaks of Amida's spare key that liberates him from the darkness of ignorance, accumulated for unknown eons of kalpas: "The door of the dungeon of my dark mind from the beginningless beginning was opened by Amida's spare key."[6] "Spare key" is a metaphor for wisdom granted to him by Amida, so that he can become liberated from the darkness of ignorance. As the Buddhist saying goes, "Light dispels in an instant the darkness of cave accumulated for thousands of years."

Nakamura is very clear about the source of his awakening—it is not himself or his efforts but the working of boundless compassion that makes it possible. Although the human proclivity is to make claims for spiritual achievement, it is nothing but pride and arrogance. Through deep hearing, Nakamura identifies the source of his liberation:

> *In the timeless process of birth-and-death,*
> *for the first time I was made to realize*
> *the Other Power of Amida Buddha.*
> *My understanding resulted from listening,*

> but listening is nothing but a little scratch
>   on a precious gem.
> I trusted my understanding instead of trusting Amida.
> Until now I was satisfied with my understanding.
> But, my understanding does not save me;
>   It is Amida who saves me.[7]

A similar appreciation for a mistakenly placed trust in oneself, rather than in boundless compassion, comes in the confessional of Chiyono Sasaki. She was one of the leading lay persons who helped people in the Kona area to cultivate a true appreciation of NAMU-AMIDA-BUTSU. But, like Nakamura, she regrets her once-mistaken claim to faith:

> How shameful, how shameful
>   for not knowing Amida's true compassion.
> Looking at myself only, I worried and calculated
>   about this understanding and that understanding.
> I listened, believed and calculated
>   with my self-power mind,
>   not realizing that it was the self-power mind
>   that pushed true compassion away from myself.
> When I listened, I listened by relying on myself.
> When I knew, I credited myself for knowing.
> I was satisfied with myself
>   who listened, believed and learned.
> Without realizing hell waiting for me,
>   I appeared to be happy and contented.
> Without thinking about hell seriously,
>   I did not see myself as going to hell.
> In spite of false views, laziness and selfishness,
>   I was proud of myself as the person
>   who practiced selfless giving.

With the understanding which I concoct—
no way can I go to the Pure Land.[8]

Unlike the path of Sages where a person achieves wisdom, these people, lacking wisdom were granted it. The endowed wisdom enabled them to deal with difficulties in everyday living. The problem of anger, for example, is diffused by the nembutsu. In the words of Tai Oshima,

> *On the fire of revenge*
> *do not pour the oil of grudge.*
> *Instead, add the water of Dharma*
> *to extinguish the fire.*[9]

The water of Dharma here is NAMU–AMIDA–BUTSU. Anger is diminished when one realizes that one is a foolish being, as the other might also be, both within boundless compassion. The situation is assessed more or less objectively and dealt with expeditiously. That one is a foolish being caught in the web of karmic bondage is a realization that comes naturally only within the bosom of boundless, nonjudgmental compassion. Each of us is primarily responsible for the consequences of past karmic life, grateful that we no longer create seeds for future suffering. Mrs. Oshima's husband, Jutaro Oshima, makes this point when he writes:

> *Evils, faults, dirt and trash*
> *that I accumulate day after day*
> NAMU–AMIDA–BUTSU *is a broom*
> *sweeping them away.*[10]

Here the nembutsu is likened to a broomstick that sweeps away the defilements of ego-self. One of the most important qualities imparted by the nembutsu is the reflection that provides a check against self-righteousness. There is no greater arrogance than thinking that one is always right. This appears in countless subtle forms, surfacing beyond our conscious control.

Haru Matsuda had many children, worked hard in the Kona coffee fields, and devoted her life to deep hearing. She admonishes herself, rather than others, for her shortcomings illuminated by the wisdom granted her in the nembutsu:

> *While telling my children*
> *not to criticize others,*
> *I speak ill*
> *of others.*[11]

The life of nembutsu, above all, manifests what it means to be truly human. When she was informed by the United States military in World War II that her son had died fighting for his country on the battlefields of Europe, she wrote:

> *Being asked by my remaining children*
> *whether I felt lonely,*
> *I say, "I'm just fine,"*
> *As teardrops appear.*

Her son was a member of the celebrated 442nd Combat Battalion, the most decorated unit in American military history. Within boundless compassion, she is permitted to openly weep, even though she wishes not to show it to her young children.

Summing up her Shin Buddhist life are two more poems by Haru Matsuda, touching on both the level of everyday living and on the deeper one of religious awakening.

> *Embraced by* NAMU-AMIDA-BUTSU,
> *I vowed never to complain.*

> *Thinking thus,*
> *again I complained.*

Having awakened to the world of boundless compassion, she vowed, in spite of her harsh and burdensome life, never to complain. Yet the moment she had thus thought, she began grumbling about the demanding day ahead. People might criticize her for her weakness, but it is also stark reality. That she is able to freely and openly complain about the day's work is made possible within boundless compassion that does not judge but embraces her just as she is.

This is the reason that she also demonstrates a profound appreciation for the vertical, depth dimension of life breaking through the horizontal plane of everyday life:

> *Rubbing my eyes in the morning,*
> *I'm complaining again.*
> *Out jumped* NAMU–AMIDA–BUTSU
> *and I really woke up.*

When the nembutsu jumped out of her mouth, Mrs. Matsuda awakens in a twofold sense. Her eyes open, she wakes up, gathers her strength, and prepares for the hard day ahead with a firm determination (horizontal plane). But at the same time she also wakes up to realize her place in the cosmic scheme of things and to the profound appreciation for this unrepeatable life (vertical dimension). She realizes herself as *namu,* a limited karma-bound self, within the bosom of boundless compassion that is *amida-butsu.*

One of the well-known products of this Shin community in Kona was Ellison Onizuka, the first Buddhist and first Asian American astronaut, who died tragically in the Challenger space shuttle explosion of January 28, 1986. Upon returning from one of his earlier secret military flights around the globe, Ellison told his mother how astonished he was to see from outer space that Earth had no boundaries of any kind. We could say that in one sense he saw the Pure Land, because as defined by T'an-luan in the sixth century, the Pure Land is "infinite, like space, vast and boundless."[12] Since it has no boundaries, the Pure Land is everywhere. In fact, it is never apart from the very place where we stand at this very moment, although it is beyond ordinary consciousness.

17

Personal and Social

The light of boundless compassion not only illuminates our existential reality of karmic evil, but
its warm rays and nurturing power transforms it
completely into the highest good, with social implications. In fact, the deeper the spirituality and self-
actualization, the greater the concern shown for
social action and change.[1] This has been true in the
long history of Shin Buddhism in Japan, which has
been at the forefront of social consciousness and
political action, as amply documented by Galen Amstutz

in his book *Interpreting Amida: History and Orientalism in the Study of Pure Land Buddhism*. The challenge for American Shin Buddhists is clearly set forth in this study, but our task here is to clarify the creative basis for social action emerging from spiritual and religious transformation.

The core of personal transformation is clarified by Shinran when he states:

> To be transformed means that evil karma without being nullified and eradicated is made into the highest good, just as all river waters, upon entering the great ocean, immediately become ocean water.[2]

Here the transformation is not simply a matter of A being turned into B; a radical change is involved, whereby A remains A and yet it becomes B. This is inconceivable from the standpoint of self-power, but it is most natural and logical as the working of the invisible Other Power that operates in a seamless universe.

Shinran explains this transformation by various metaphors, the most well known being the process of ice becoming water. It is not the case that ice is discarded and then water obtained; rather, ice remains ice and for that very reason water is obtained. If we got rid of ice, there would be no water. Another frequently cited example is the fresh river water, flowing from higher elevation and meandering into the ocean, that becomes salt water. The river water does not change itself into salt water before entering the sea, but when it does flow into the ocean, it naturally becomes salt water.

In Japan, where persimmons are abundant in autumn, this transformation is likened to the bitterness of an unripened persimmon that naturally becomes sweetness in the ripening process. It is not the case that the bitter taste is extracted before the sweet taste appears; the natural process of ripening transforms the bitterness itself into sweetness. No external power is involved, for it comes about by itself, of its own accord.

The consequence of transformation by virtue of boundless compassion turns a person of karmic evil to lead a moral life naturally and spontaneously. This may seem contradictory, for karmic evil would appear to go against the good, whatever that may mean, but the truth of the matter is the exact opposite. According to Shinran, "Even though we may do evil, even more should we think about the power of the Vow. Then, tenderness and forbearance will appear by virtue of 'made to become so by itself,' (that is, naturally and spontaneously)."[3]

One of the potential misunderstandings of Shin Buddhism since the time of Shinran in the thirteenth century is the heresy of licensed evil (*zoaku-muge*), a phenomenon found in all world religions under the name of antinomianism. In the Shin case, proponents have argued that if Amida Buddha's compassion is directed to saving the evildoer, then we can commit evil and still be saved. Some even conclude that not to commit evil shows complete lack of faith in the working of absolute compassion.

Shinran points out the fallacy of such a belief in extant letters addressed to his disciples. In a letter dated the eighth month, nineteenth day, 1252, he writes to a disciple, "How lamentable that people who have not fully awakened from drunkenness are urged to more drunkenness and those still in the grips of poison encouraged yet to take more poison. . . . 'Here's some medicine, so drink all the poison you like'—words like this should never be said."[4] While the fallacy of licensed evil can be easily refuted, some followers doubted their ability to do good, since they had been taught that they were filled with nothing but delusions. To such people Shinran teaches that boundless compassion, directed especially to those who become aware of their limited, imperfect, and vulnerable self, brings about a profound change in their attitude to the world:

In people who have long heard the Buddha's Name and said the nembutsu, surely there are signs of rejecting the evil of this world and signs of their desire to cast off the evil in themselves. . . . Such a person then joyfully says the Name of Amida Buddha deeply entrusting the self to the Vow. That people seek to stop doing wrong as the heart moves them, although earlier they gave thought to such things and committed them as their minds dictated, is surely a sign of having rejected the world.[5]

In truly entrusting oneself to boundless compassion, people naturally and spontaneously reject the world and its proclivities for evil, and "seek to stop doing wrong as the heart moves them."

The highest moral life and the truly religious life are inseparable, and both are characterized by humility, repentance, and gratitude. Since the truly religious or spiritual life affirms the reality of human finitude—whether called evil, sin, foolishness, or darkness of ignorance—the consequence for an ethical life is that one acts with humility and identifies with the lowliest in society—the neglected and downtrodden, the weak and disabled, the disenfranchised and excluded. And rather than trying to "save" them from a superior, privileged position, one serves them by affirming their dignity, self-worth, and human potential.

This is the reason that repentance is central to the moral and ethical life. This means to confess not only to one's limitations to do good but also to lament that one can never do enough. I once read an account by Fumio Sato, the Japanese actor who played the role of Chiune Sugihara five hundred times on stage. Sugihara was the Japanese consul in Kaunas, Lithuania, in 1941, who sacrificed his professional life as a diplomat to save thousands of Jewish lives by issuing exit visas against the order of his own government in Tokyo. Reminiscing about his role as a good Samaritan, Sato states, "Sugihara saved a lot of Jewish people. But at the same time he couldn't save a lot of Jews. I try my best to depict his feelings toward those he couldn't save."[6]

Repentance minimizes the possibility of self-indulgence and self-righteousness when performing good by helping others. Although we cannot go into it here, the Buddhist rituals of repentance cover both commissions and omissions in one's countless past lives.

The center of power is reversed when social ethics are rooted in the truly religious life. The one who gives is the one who benefits; the one who teaches is the one who is taught; the one who saves is the one who is saved. Gratitude, then, becomes an essential component of the ethical life. Humility, repentance, and gratitude are crucial for any social action that is true, real, and sincere.

樹心弘誓佛地

泳念難思法海

PART THREE

Life as Creative Act

18

Creativity in Shin Life

The Shin Buddhist path may be summed up in three phases: descriptive, evocative, and creative. Buddhism, including Shin, does not give clear and firm directives for everyday living. It is not prescriptive. Nor does it have solutions to every social problem confronting us. Its utility value is not a compelling concern. Rather, the basic teachings recognize suffering as it is and probe the source of suffering. It is primarily descriptive. By awakening to reality as-it-is and shattering false constructs about self and world, a person is on the right path to wisdom and compassion, and it may be used to change oneself and the world.

This basic approach inherits the legacy of the historical Buddha, who formulated the Four Noble Truths according to the prevailing model of medical science. The diagnosis of the human condition reveals that life does not move according to one's wishes (First Noble Truth of Suffering) and that the root cause is insatiable and unrealistic desires of the ego-self (Second Noble Truth). The prognosis describes the healthy state of human life where we develop our fullest potential (Third Noble Truth) and outlines a method to achieve that optimum state of health (Fourth Noble Truth).

That the descriptive is the basis of Buddhist life is evident, for example, in the First Noble Truth. We all suffer from the four basic experiences of birth, old age, illness, and death, none of which we can control. In addition, we suffer when we have to be with people we dislike, when we become separated from loved ones, whether in life or in death, when we fail to obtain the object of our desire, and when we grasp the ever-changing, conditioned self as permanent. This insight into life's reality makes us reflect deeply on the true nature of self and world, beyond a commonsense acceptance of the way things are.

The second phase, which I call evocative, brings to our awareness two interrelated dimensions of life normally neglected or overlooked: the insatiable activity of the ego-self and the boundless compassion that illuminates it. In philosophical language it describes the relationship between the finite and the infinite. This dual awareness is latent in every human being, but the goal of the Buddhist is the transformation of blind passions into the content of enlightenment. Since blind passion is said to be rooted in countless past lives, its transformation requires the working of boundless compassion over many kalpas or eons of timeless time.

The descriptive and the evocative are realized progressively on the religious path, through an inner transformation. But the third

and final stage of the Shin path, the creative, occurs in our interaction with the world. Critical life situations challenge us to respond with our whole being and not with ready-made answers.
Thus, a new and unique self is born with each changing situation
and demand that confronts us. One's life itself then becomes a
work of art reminiscent of the ultimate goal of Nietzsche's Will to
Power as advocated in his *Birth of Tragedy*.

When the modern Japanese philosopher Kitaro Nishida ana-
lyzed the creative act, he coined a term "action–intuition" (*koiteki-
chokkan*). This means that reality gives rise to an intuition on the
part of an artist, who then reacts to create and fashion a response.
It is not the case that an artist first has some kind of subjective inspiration that leads to creating a work of art. Rather, the reverse
takes place. The raw material of the world itself supplies resources
for the artist's vision and creativity. This process was articulated by
Basho, the founder of the haiku poetic tradition, as noted by one
of his disciples:

> Go to the pine if you want to learn about the pine, or to the
> bamboo if you want to learn about the bamboo. And in
> doing so, you must leave your subjective preoccupation
> with yourself. Otherwise you impose yourself on the object
> and do not learn. Your poetry issues of its own accord when
> you and the object have become one—when you have
> plunged deep enough into the object to see something like
> a hidden glimmering there.[1]

A good poem about a pine or a bamboo emerges only when
we leave behind our preconceptions and expectations, and we let
the object speak for itself through us. The groundwork, of course,
has been laid down by years of study, training, and self-discipline
in perfecting the craft of haiku poetry. What is to be avoided is poetry that is nothing but one's subjectivity. Basho's own words conclude the above quotation:

However well phrased your poetry may be, if your feeling is not natural—if the object and yourself are separate—then your poetry is not true poetry but your subjective counterfeit.

Since Buddhism is primarily descriptive and not prescriptive, each person is challenged to respond creatively to a given situation. Whatever that challenge may be—whether physical, mental, social, institutional, or historical—we face reality as it is, realizing our limited, imperfect, vulnerable, and mortal self, which is sustained by boundless compassion. On that basis we proceed to respond creatively to the world, coming up with solutions unique to the problem at hand.

The essence of nembutsu, NAMU-AMIDA-BUTSU, is the constant renewal of the *namu*-self as a creative act. This is an ongoing process, continuing as long as we live this human life. Obviously, it is not a static state, built on egocentric clinging to things, but a dynamic fashioning of a constantly evolving self. That is foundational to the Zen ideal, "Wherever you stand, you become the master." What does it mean to be one's own master? A simple example may help us here.

When I first started taking private lessons in aikido at its world headquarters in Tokyo, my teacher, the late Akira Tohei, reminded me that aikido is not simply a matter of mastering self-defense techniques but of finding one's own center and manifesting an autonomous self in everyday life. When I was anxious about taking my very first promotion test, Tohei Sensei reminded me that the instructors not only watch the student's mastery of a given technique, but they also carefully observe the demeanor from beginning to end—how one sits, stands, bows, and faces a partner before executing a technique, and afterward how one sits, bows, and returns to the original place on the mat.

I understood this to mean that I must be my total self completely, not concerned about techniques, or comparing myself to others, or trying to gain the promotion. The full implications of Tohei Sensei's advice came to me much later, when I was forced to practice aikido with different teachers.

Once, when Tohei Sensei was away to conduct a week-long retreat, his replacement, another professional instructor on the headquarters staff, came to teach. When he asked me to perform certain movements, I would do so as I had diligently practiced with my own teacher many times. But the substitute teacher would correct me and make me execute it according to his own style. This was very frustrating, and I thought to myself, Why don't the teachers get together and agree on a uniform method of teaching? After all, they're the same techniques. In fact, they even seemed to contradict each other when it came to the proper stance, speed of each movement, arc of spherical motions, and the different points of emphasis.

I became even more frustrated when a third substitute teacher came to class one day and again taught an entirely different way to execute the same techniques. So one day I complained to Tohei Sensei, saying "Why can't the teachers, all professionals on the same staff, agree on the teaching methods, instead of each one making students learn all kinds of different styles? It's not only frustrating but also counterproductive."

I don't recall what my teacher said, but it soon dawned on me that my task as a student was to learn precisely what the different teachers taught me, each in his own way, even if they differed among themselves. Absorbing as much as possible the instructions received from various teachers, I have to develop my own style— forged by my temperament, physical capabilities, and limited athleticism. I must not be a second-hand copy of any of my teachers. Only in this way can I respond creatively to any situation.

A similar kind of creativity is found in the path of nembutsu, for each of us as *namu* is given the ability and freedom within the boundless space that is *amida-butsu* to become what we are as original and unique individuals. Such an accomplishment is not limited only to the personal and spiritual spheres but also applies to our social and ethical life. These aspects of the self cannot be easily differentiated, for we are talking about the total person. That the truly ethical person must also be creative is affirmed by Rabindranath Tagore when he writes:

> Civility is beauty of behaviour. It requires for its perfection patience, self-control, and an environment of leisure. For genuine courtesy is a creation, like pictures, like music. It is a harmonious blending of voice, gesture and movement, words and action, in which generosity of conduct is expressed. It reveals the man himself and has no ulterior purpose.[2]

The Buddhist tradition challenges each of us to become more than what we are as a limited karmic being, to reveal the potential that awaits to be creatively expressed. We are reminded of this lifelong responsibility when we turn to the symbolism of the *stupa* of five elemental rings crowned by "space" (*akasha*).

19

Space as Metaphor

A familiar sight when visiting Buddhist temple compounds in Japan is the tombstone, known as *gorinto,*
the *stupa* of five rings. It is a votive memorial with
five layers of various sizes of stone or granite, symbolizing the basic elements that constitute life—earth,
water, fire, ether, and space. Placed in ascending
order from the bottom, they are the square base
(earth), a sphere (water), a pyramid (fire), an inverted
hemisphere (air or wind), and a round ball, *chinta-
mani* (space). The first four are said to symbolize, re-

spectively, mass, liquid, heat, and energy, but what about space? What is the significance of space? Why does it crown the stupa?

Stupas originated in ancient India as burial mounds of the famous and powerful. When the historical Buddha passed away at Kushinagara, his cremated remains were distributed to eight kingdoms, with two more added later, and ultimately a total of ten stupas were built to enshrine his remains. They became objects of veneration and worship, the center of lay Buddhist religious life. Circumambulation of the stupas became a major form of ritual worship. As the popularity of stupa worship grew among the laity, they were incorporated into the monastic compounds, and stupas became venerated as the physical presence of the Buddha. Later in history stupa architecture underwent various transformations, especially as it moved from India to the East Asian cultural spheres. In Tibet the stupa evolved into the *chorten,* and in China, Korea, and Japan it became the many-tiered pagodas.

The miniature versions of stupas were widely disseminated as votary objects and ritual implements. The erection of these stupas were believed to accrue merits for the donor, equal to those gained by commissioning Buddhist sculptures or patronizing the erection of temples. Soon they evolved into the five-tiered tombstones that became popular in Japan from the ninth century, especially with the spread of esoteric Shingon and Tendai Buddhism, which regarded the five-ringed pagoda, called *sotoba,* as the very body of Vairochana Buddha.

We find references to the four basic elements of earth, water, fire, and air in many cultures, such as the pre-Socratics in Greece, the materialist school in India, the philosophical schools of China, and so on, but it is generally in the Hindu and Buddhist tradition that we find an emphasis on the fifth element, space, or *akasha.*

The definition of *akasha* is "free, open space, vacuity" or "that which is all-pervading, infinite, and without origin." It is the boundless space beyond our linguistically constructed world, which is characterized by divisions of all kinds. It is contrasted to

Space as Metaphor

another Sanskrit term, *antariksha* which also means space, but this term is used in ordinary discourse, when, for example, we speak of personal space, parking space, outer space, sacred space, empty space, or blank space. These spaces are human constructs that have arbitrary boundaries that are subject to change. In addition, there is a third sense of space that we cannot go into here: aesthetic space, an essential component found in Chinese and Japanese calligraphy, monochrome painting, Japanese flower arranging, architecture, Noh dance, and other art forms.

In the Hindu classic *Chandogya Upanishad,* the space between the sky and earth is denoted as *antariksha,* while that which upholds it is called *akasha,* boundless space.[1] The two, however, are one in the sense that *atman* and Brahman are one. This distinction is inherited in the *Lotus Sutra,* the most popular Buddhist scripture in East Asia. In the chapter called "Bodhisattvas Springing Out of the Earth," when the historical Buddha is about to pass away, celebrated bodhisattvas appear in worldly space, *antariksha,* to take on the mantle of spreading the Buddha Dharma. But the Buddha rejects them and turns to countless unknown bodhisattvas who emerge from the space below the earth, *akasha,* to carry out the mission of propagating the *Lotus Sutra.* Praising these nameless bodhisattvas, he states: "All these bodhisattvas dwell in the space beneath this world, there they read, recite, penetrate, ponder and discriminate the sutras and correctly keep them in memory."[2] The bodhisattvas who emerge from space below the earth embrace worldly space as its own and transform it spiritually.[3]

In brief, that which crowns the stupa is symbolic of the boundless space that is *akasha,* the arena for true and real life, where the creative spiritual life is consummated. This open space enables each person to become creative, forming and fashioning a truly unique self. The Buddhist path guides a person into this boundless space, providing the opportunity for self-realization in its radical sense.

We all seek boundless space, consciously or unconsciously,

where we can realize our fullest potential. The young search for it, adults yearn for it, the academics talk about it. We find this quest, for example, in the youthful songs of Loreena McKennitt, who is constantly exploring such possibilities through world music. She ponders,

> In the end, I wonder if one of the most important steps on our journey is the one in which we throw away the map. In jettisoning the grids and brambles of our own preconceptions, perhaps we are able to find the real secrets of each place; to remember that we are all extensions of our collective history.[4]

This move to go beyond preconceptions and human constructs inspired peoples from ancient times to devise various religious and spiritual strategies. The motivation is an extension of our collective karma, and we might say that it is built into the very structure of life itself. Robert Murphy, in his work *An Overture to Social Anthropology*, formulates this as follows:

> In structural theory the structure of the psyche is universally the same and the working of the mind involves a continued process of sorting one's perceptions into paired opposites, which are then reconciled. . . . the stream of consciousness becomes broken up into discrete events and things, which are usually reducible to words. . . . Words and symbols . . . allow us to break up reality and reduce it to the hard, objective status of the word.

> At the same time, it does certain violence to the human grasp on reality—the same mind that sets up these oppositions is also continually trying to mend them, to reconcile them, and to synthesize their antithesis.[5]

Deep within the human psyche there exists the need to make order out of chaos, to find meaning out of nothingness, but this is frequently undertaken purely as a conscious act. If so, it does injustice to the powerful unconscious drive for the reconciliation of opposites. The religious paths, with their doctrines, creeds, and precepts, aspire to such a reconciliation, but this too, if not properly embodied on both conscious and unconscious levels, can become "grids and brambles" themselves, obstructing our vision and hindering self-realization.

In sum, the stupa of five elemental rings reminds us that human life is made up of earth, water, fire, and air, but that it awaits to be consummated within boundless space where we *become* who we really are. Our task in life, then, is to fashion and create our unique selves in the open space of infinite possibilities where we might realize *virtue* in the sense akin to Paul Tillich's definition of the term: "the power of being and fulfillment of meaning."[6]

It should be underscored that boundless space exists not only for human beings, for it is also nature's space where all things realize their own selfhood. This is the realm of nature as it is and not nature grasped from a human-centered perspective. Such a transhuman vision drove Isamu Noguchi to see his sculptural works as part and parcel of nature:

> An unlimited field for abstract sculptural expression would then be realized in which flowers and trees, rivers and mountains, as well as birds, beasts and man, would be given their due place. Indeed, a fine balance of spirit with matter can only concur when the artist has so thoroughly submerged himself in the study of the unity of nature as to truly become once more a part of nature—a part of the very earth, thus to view the inner surfaces and the life elements.[7]

For everything to be given its due place, the human-centered standpoint must be shed. When we do so, we realize that each form of existence—human, animal, plant, flower, rock, mountain, and river—constitutes the vast network of interdependence and interconnectedness of which each is a significant part.

That the task of each form of life is to attain such a realization is already implicit in the first pronouncement made by the infant Buddha, "Above heaven and below heaven, I alone am the World-Honored One." But this personal awakening means a deeper commitment to changing the world, as demonstrated by the life of Buddha and its impact in the history of humankind.

20

The World-Honored One

Many legends surround the birth of the historical Buddha, one of which is the miraculous event that took place immediately after he was born. Legend states that the infant Buddha took seven steps in each of the four directions and, pointing one finger to the sky and the other to the earth, he proclaimed, "Above heaven and below heaven, I alone am the World-Honored One." In some accounts this is followed by the statement: "And he made sure that all beings attain the same state of bliss." This event symbolizes the Buddhist ideal that affirms the potential of each person to attain Buddhahood, the supreme embodiment of wisdom and compassion. It has nothing to do with the conventional ego-self but everything to do with the possibility hidden in all beings to attain the same dignity, self-worth, and self-reliance as the historical Buddha. This universal affirmation is symbolized by the magnificent garland of flowers placed on the universe at the very moment of his supreme enlightenment, as expounded in the *Avatamsaka Sutra,* or the *Flower Garland Sutra.*

But this event contains another significant message about the religious life. The "I" that Buddha refers to is not the subject in relation to an object; it is not an I that can be replaced by any other I. It is what some philosophers call Existenz, the Subject that is absolutely unique and irreplaceable. This comes about by taking the seventh step, transcending the delusory, dichotomous I that is transmigrating in the six realms of hell, hungry ghosts, animals, fighting demons, human beings, and heavenly beings. The seventh step means the liberation and freedom from this cycle of endless rebirths. The title World-Honored One is bestowed upon anyone who takes the seventh step. Many enlightened people before Shakyamuni Buddha attained such a liberation, but he was the first to articulate it and make it available to everyone in our historical world system.

Here we must pause and distinguish between two different senses of the first-person pronoun "I": the dualistic sense of I used in ordinary discourse, and the nondualistic sense of I that is found in the Buddha's proclamation.

The dualistic or conventional I believes itself to be self-sufficient; it is unaware that it is a fictive self driven by self-centered blind passions. The historical Buddha, influenced by many factors, both known and unknown, turned inward and sought liberation and freedom from such a deluded self. After six years of immense spiritual struggle, he attained supreme enlightenment. His first proclamation after his awakening identifies the radical self-delusion at the core of our conventional life. Called the Song of Victory, the Buddha declares:

> *I ran through* samsara, *with its many births,*
> *Searching for, but not finding, the house-builder.*
> *Misery is birth again and again.*
>
> *House builder, you are seen!*
> *The house you shall not build again!*
> *Broken are your rafters, all,*
> *Your roof beam destroyed.*
> *Freedom from the* samkharas *has the mind attained.*
> *To the end of cravings has it come.*[1]

The "house-builder" is the ego-self that builds a protective wall around itself. It is said to be motivated by *samkharas,* which are instinctual, subconscious forces. Liberation from the house-builder makes possible a newly realized self that is interrelated and interconnected with all beings. The legacy of the historical Buddha down through the centuries has focused on the dismantling of this house-builder, by means of diverse methods and practices. Among them, the Pure Land tradition teaches that this is done through the working of boundless compassion which nullifies and transforms the ego-self into its opposite.

This dualistic I may also be a challenge in the Christian tradition. In the preface to the religious classic *Theologia Germanica,* Bengt Hagglund writes:

There is *one* mighty hindrance for everybody to lead a good life in a right relation to God and to his neighbor, i.e. in a true love. The name of this fundamental evil is "I" and "mine" and "me."[2]

He concludes with the command, "My many words on the subject can be summed up by a few: Cut off our self, cleanly and utterly."

In Buddhism to "cut off our self, cleanly and utterly" means the realization of a newly awakened I that is interrelated and interconnected with all beings. In this vast web of interdependence, the title the World-Honored One is bestowed on anyone who has awakened to this true and real, nondualistic self. It should be underscored that in the famous injunctions of the Buddha to his disciples, "Be ye lamps (*dipa*) unto yourself," or "Be ye islands (*dvipa*) unto your self," the references are to the nondualistic self that manifests *dhamma,* "things, including the self, as they are." This self, then, is not the isolated, dualistic I but the nondualistic I that "holds fast to the *dhamma* as a lamp." Here, the self and *dhamma* co-exist in double exposure; hence, it has nothing to do with the conventional ego-self.[3]

The same affirmation of personhood is also expressed by Shinran, but he does so in the language of the Pure Land tradition. In the epilogue to the *Tannisho* he states: "When I ponder on the compassionate Vow of Amida, established through five kalpas of profound thought, I realize that it was for myself, Shinran, alone."[4] The phrase "Shinran alone" is not exclusionary, making a claim only for himself. Rather, it is an affirmation available to anyone who awakens to the boundless compassion that is Amida Buddha, for whom each form of life is, as it were, his only child. Thus, every Shin person who engages in deep hearing can replace "Shinran" with his or her own name to proclaim, "The compassionate Vow of Amida is for myself alone."

21

The Ordinary as Extraordinary

The affirmation of true personhood in a world of interdependence and interconnectedness also affirms the dignity of all things, both animate and inanimate, as being of supreme importance. In fact, dharma in the primary sense, differentiated from dharma as teaching, connotes that each person, each thing, and each event, no matter how seemingly insignificant, contains extraordinary meaning and priceless value. Many lay Shin Buddhists have left us countless poems that make this point, perceiving the working of true compassion in a single stone or in a single blade of grass. In the words of the myokonin Ichitaro,

> The Land of Bliss is found everywhere. On a vegetable leaf. On a blade of grass. On a sardine. Without saying whether a thing is good or bad, if you sense the working of Amida in and on each thing, this is the truth freed of good and bad of things. All good and bad are the products of one's thoughts. Namu-amida-butsu.[1]

I once had a dream in which I was wading in a wide, shallow river with the water coming up to my knees. It was a strikingly beautiful day—the water clear and pure, the air crisp and energizing, the sky deep and blue, the sunshine warm and exhilarating. When I looked around, I saw that both river banks were made of lush foliage, sculpted as though an expert gardener had given them a smooth, curving shape, rising higher than a two-story house.

Then, looking around on both banks, I suddenly noticed small niches in the midst of the foliage, set equidistant from each other. They appeared to contain statues of some sort. And when I looked closely, on one side I saw figures of the Bodhisattva of Compassion, Avalokiteshvara, known as Kuan-yin or Kannon in East Asia, and on the other side I noticed statues of similar shape and form that I recognized as the Virgin Mary. I sensed some kind of epiphany coming; my heart was pounding filled with anticipation. The whole atmosphere quivered with religious significance. The scene was filled with spiritual energy, nature was vibrant, the feminine exuded abundant life.

While I was dreaming, I was also doing self-analysis. Cool clear water suggests a rich subconscious in which I wade knee high, enjoying every moment. The blue sky without a speck of cloud suggests clarity of consciousness, free of the clouds of delusion. The sound of the rippling stream is soothing and comforting. The rich foliage gives off exuberant energy. The feminine symbols from

East and West, enclosed in the niches, emanate love that knows no boundaries. They both watch over me, as if to bless a rare spiritual event about to occur.

Filled with anticipation, I look around and notice something glimmering in the riverbed. It glitters as the sunlight dances on the rippling water. I stoop down, move the pebbles away, and pick up the object—a one-pound can of Hills Brothers coffee! What a disappointment! The most mundane thing in my life! An avid coffee lover at that time, I used to drink at least a dozen cups of coffee a day.

In my dejection, I hold up the coffee can and then remove the lid. Lo! And behold! It's filled with tasty crabmeat, my favorite food! Delicious and sweet crabmeat is nourishing and uplifting; it fills my being with energy and life and joy. As I savor the taste of crabmeat, my eyes open and I wake up.

This dream reminds me once again that the highest religious and spiritual life is to be found in the very midst of everyday, mundane reality and not in some form of transcendence apart from our world as we know it. Our task in life is to discover that which is extraordinary in the most ordinary mundane things. The object of our spiritual quest may be right here before us, if only we have eyes to see.

22

Two Parables

Forming the background of Shin Buddhism and hidden under the surface simplicity of its teachings are two major cultural characteristics of Asian civilization. One is the depth analysis of human consciousness developed in the Abhidharma and Yogachara schools of Buddhism, which forms the foundation for the Shin insight into the deluded self. The other is the tradition of self-cultivation in the ethical, aesthetic, and religious spheres that Shin Buddhism also inherits, forming what I call the interior practice of nembutsu life.[1]

The simplicity of the Shin Buddhist path conceals the inner struggle for meaning, whereby a person devotes himself or herself to deep hearing. It is not obvious to an outsider, but one pursues deep hearing in the manner of self-cultivation. This is a basic component in Shin life, although never fully articulated, because it can be counterproductive.

What we mean by self-cultivation in the religious life can be illustrated by contrasting the thrust of two parables, Christian and Buddhist, which have a similar structure but different messages: the parable of the prodigal son in the Gospel according to Luke (15:11–32) and the parable of the Wealthy Merchant and his Beggar Son in the *Lotus Sutra*.[2]

The New Testament parable involves a father who has two sons. The younger son receives his share of the inheritance, but he squanders everything as soon as he receives it from his father. Destitute and with nowhere to go, he decides to return home to his father. When he confesses his sins and admits to his unworthiness, he is welcomed back into the fold, and the father forgives and embraces him, providing the best robe, shoes, and ring, and orders that a grand feast be held to celebrate his return. The older brother, who has led an exemplary life, serving his father and never disobeying him, becomes upset, because he feels that he is the more deserving of such accolade and honor. But the father praises the younger son, saying, "It was fitting to make merry and be glad, for this your brother was dead, and is alive; he was lost, and is found." (Luke 15:32). This demonstrates the love of a forgiving God, favoring the younger son who has confessed his culpability. Immediate salvation is assured for the sinful and repentant.

The parable from the *Lotus Sutra* has a similar motif but with a significant difference. It involves a wealthy man who lives in luxury but lacks an heir. His only son left home as a youth, led a wandering and profligate life, and now lives in poverty as a beggar. As the father grows old, he searches for his long-lost son, whom he has not seen in fifty years, so that his wealth can be passed on to him. When the son comes looking for work at his father's mansion, he is overwhelmed with its splendor, wealth, and countless servants and feels completely out of place. The son doesn't know that it's his own father's house, but the father recognizes him immediately and wants to welcome him back. But, fearful that his son may be scared away, overwhelmed by the splendor of the mansion, the father devises a plan to bring him back into the household. He first hires the beggar as a laborer, gradually gives him more responsibilities, and slowly promotes him by giving him important duties. The son works hard, gains the trust of the staff, and finally is promoted to the highest post among the hired hands.

On his deathbed, the wealthy man announces that this worker is really his son who shall inherit the estate from him. The son, gaining something totally unexpected, rejoices and says, "Without any mind for or effort on my part these treasures now come of themselves to me."[3] Although he has worked hard and earned his place as the foremost worker in the household, he disclaims any credit.

The wealthy man is the Buddha, and the long-lost son is each of us. Although we are told that we are the primary recipients of boundless compassion, that the wealth of the world is ours to have, we do not believe it or accept it. But in due course of time, as our understanding is nurtured through the interior practice of deep hearing, we arrive at a stage where we are ready to gratefully accept the Buddha's compassion.

Both stories illustrate the working of love and compassion in a profound way, yet there is a major difference between the two. In the parable of the prodigal son, the confession of sin leads to immediate salvation resulting from God's mercy. In the Buddhist story, a process of awakening and discovery is required, such that one comes to know intimately the saving powers of the Buddha's compassion, as well as its reason for focusing on the being of karmic limitations. It is not the case that compassion is being withheld; rather, it suggests that spiritual maturity is required for us to accept the compassion of the Buddha without doubt or hesitation.

When we compare the two parables, it is easy to focus on their similarity, but the difference reflects the cultural context of the respective traditions: an omnipotent and omniscient God that rules over the destiny of human beings on the one hand, and the Buddha of boundless compassion that nurtures spirituality according to each person's karmic history on the other. If and when we are fortunate to fully awaken to the working of boundless compassion, we ascribe it to our "good karmic past" (*shukuen*). If the process takes longer for some of us, we know that it is due to karmic circumstances beyond our control, but we must continue to strive until the conditions ripen for our awakening. The relentless working of boundless compassion will never cease until everyone achieves final liberation and freedom.

23

Life as Naturalness: Jinen

The ultimate goal of Pure Land Buddhism was summed up by Honen when he said,

> Flames rise to the sky, water flows downward. Among fruits there are those that are sour and those that are sweet. All this is according to the logic of naturalness (*jinen*).[1]

These are obvious facts in the natural world, and "logic" here simply points to things, including the self, as they are. But we human beings find it immensely difficult to align ourselves with just the way things are. *Jinen* is impossible to render into English, and "naturalness" may be the closest English equivalent, but it is not a primitive state of being, nor is it identical with Rousseau's natural impulse. In fact, *jinen* is the highest state of being achieved by human consciousness liberated from the calculating ego-self. That is, one *becomes* naturalness through effort and dedication until the state of effortlessness is realized. Honen's naturalness resonates with a story of Patacara, a nun from the Pali scriptures of early Buddhism.

One day Patacara finds herself despondent, when she compares herself to a man who works hard in the fields, plowing the land, planting the seeds, harvesting his crops, acquiring wealth, and raising a large and happy family. He gets results and is rewarded for his hard work. Why, she asks herself, cannot I get results and attain my goal in the religious life? Patacara is confused and lost, but suddenly a turning-of-the-mind occurs when she experiences water flowing downward. In her words,

> Having washed my feet, I paid attention to the waters; and seeing the foot-water come to the low land from the high land (flowing downhill), then I concentrated my mind, like a noble thoroughbred horse.

> Then taking the lamp I entered my cell. Having inspected the bed, I sat on the couch. Then taking a needle I drew out the wick. The complete release of my mind was the quenching of the lamp.[2]

Here Patacara awakens to the natural flow of water; then she concentrates her mind on things, including the self, as they are. Her years of spiritual quest then reaches an apex; thus, with the quenching of the lamp, her thirst for results in her religious practice is also quenched. Every moment, here and now, abounds with meaning and significance.

A good contrast to Patacara is the disciple named Malunkyaputta, whose main focus is metaphysical and not the goal
of naturalness. In the famous parable of the poison arrow,
Shakyamuni Buddha remains silent about metaphysical questions.
Scholars have speculated about his silence and have given various
theories. Some say that he refused to engage in metaphysical questions that could not be verified by experience, others that he
wished to avoid disputes that would only aggravate ego-conflicts.
Still others state that he sought to underscore the practical nature
of his teaching with emphasis on conduct (*carana*) and on walking
the path (*marga*).

Now, Malunkyaputta is unhappy with the Sangha and decides
to leave the order. His primary reason for wanting to leave is that
the Buddha never takes up important questions that other contemporary teachers are discussing. They include such questions as
the following:

> That the world is eternal, that the world is not eternal, that
> the world is finite, that the world is infinite, that the soul
> and the body are identical, that the soul is one thing and the
> body another, that the saint exists after death, that the saint
> does not exist after death, that the saint both exists and does
> not exist after death, that the saint neither exists nor does not
> exist after death—these the Blessed One does not explain
> to me.[3]

When Malunkyaputta confronts the Buddha, he replies with a
parable. If shot by a poison arrow, the Buddha asks, would you
have a physician extract it immediately, or would you insist on first
getting an answer to such questions as, Who shot the poison
arrow, what was the poison made of, from which tribe did he
come, and so on without end? That would be like pursuing metaphysical questions all your life without ever getting any answers.
The task of the Buddha Dharma is to identify human suffering, its

cause, its cessation, and the way to achieve that cessation. Even if metaphysical questions are fully answered, they can never solve the problems of living and dying. Honen's proclamation—"flames rise to the sky, water flows downward"—concludes with the words,

> Since the Primal Vow of Amida vows that all sentient beings of karmic evil will be guided by the sacred Name, if a person says, "Namu-amida-butsu" singleheartedly, the welcome of the Buddha is naturally realized according to the principle of naturalness (*ho-ni*).[4]

Shinran inherits his teacher's exposition, but he gives his own understanding of naturalness in a tract called *Jinen-honi,* written at the age of eighty-six. Giving a fuller explanation of this phrase, Shinran writes:

> *Ji* means "of itself"—not through the practicer's calculation. It signifies being made so. *Nen* means "to be made so"—it is not through the practicer's calculation; it is through the working of the Tathagata's Vow.[5]

As for *honi,* another term for naturalness, he underscores the working of the Primal Vow:

> *Honi* signifies being made so through the working of the Tathagata's Vow. It is the working of the Vow where there is no room for calculation on the part of the practicer. Know, therefore, that in Other Power, no working is true working.[6]

The life of naturalness is to be lived and not discussed or debated. Jorge Luis Borges helps us understand what this means, when he writes:

A man cultivates his garden, as Voltaire wished.
He who is grateful for the existence of music.
He who takes pleasure in tracing an etymology.
Two workmen playing, in a cafe in the South,
*   a silent game of chess.*
The potter, contemplating a color and a form.
The typographer who sets this page well,
*   though it may not please him.*
A woman and a man, who read the last tercets
*   of a certain canto.*
He who strokes a sleeping animal.
He who justifies, or wishes to, a wrong done him.
He who is grateful for the existence of Stevenson.
He who prefers others to be right.
These people, unaware, are saving the world.[7]

In Buddhist terms the final stage of religious life is the realization, according to the myokonin Ichitaro, that "unenlightened ordinary man becomes an unenlightened ordinary man."[8] A similar
point is made by the great Zen teacher Kodo Sawaki: "No matter
how many years you sit doing zazen, you will never become anything special."[9]

No pretense, no angst, just the self becoming itself. All this relates to what Chuang-tzu once said:

You forget your feet when the shoes are comfortable.
You forget your waist when the belt is comfortable. Understanding forgets right and wrong when the mind is comfortable. There is no change in what is inside, no following what
is outside, when the adjustment to events is comfortable. You
begin with what is comfortable and never experience what is
uncomfortable when you know the comfort of forgetting
what is comfortable.[10]

After asserting that "Amida Buddha fulfills the purpose of making us know the significance of *jinen*," Shinran concludes his tract:

> After we have realized this, we should not be forever talking about *jinen*. If we continuously discuss *jinen*, that no working is true working will again become a working. It is a matter of inconceivable Buddha-wisdom.[11]

24

Life Beyond Our Control

The first of the Four Noble Truths of Buddhism is that life is *duhkha*. This Sanskrit word is composed of two parts: *duh* meaning bad or poor, and *kha* meaning opening, hole, or axle hole. Together it suggests a bad axle hole that makes a harsh, grating noise when the wheel turns. When life does not go smoothly, we experience the First Noble Truth of duhkha, which is frequently translated into English as "suffering." It covers, however, a much wider range of human experience, so I prefer to explain the First Noble Truth as "life does not go according to one's wish."

The antonym of *duhkha* is *sukha* (*su* means good, happy, blissful), suggesting the possibility of life evolving smoothly as it should. The compound form, *sukhavati,* or the "Land of Bliss" in Sanskrit, was loosely rendered into Chinese as "Pure Land." The Pure Land teaching has always been part of Mahayana Buddhism, and its main purpose is to counter life as *duhkha.*

While it is little known and frequently misunderstood in the West, Pure Land Buddhism has had major impact on Japanese life throughout history. That it remains an important influence even today is evident in the recent best-seller *Tariki: Embracing Despair, Discovering Peace* by Hiroyuki Itsuki, one of the leading contemporary writers in Japan. In this work the author sums up the Pure Land tradition as follows:

> (Shin Buddhism) does not tell us to try to get rid of obstructions and desires. . . . It is a religion of true and full acceptance. Because one accepts reality, it becomes clear, and pursuing it with a new clarity one arrives at truth. From there is born a true and quiet strength.

> A feeling of complete powerlessness is needed here, a disillusionment with the self, disaffection with others, and the feeling that one is, here and now, in hell. The philosophy of Absolute Other Power is the response to this state. At such a point, any faith in the self disappears without a trace. One may fight with invincible will against illness and win out, but we are all fated to die in the end, of some disease or other. There is no lasting victory. All victories are only temporary, the triumph of the moment.[1]

We must all face the reality that we have no control over birth, old age, illness, and death, especially the inevitable fact that "we are fated to die in the end, of some disease or other. There is no lasting victory."

A few years ago a colleague asked us to help her friends, a husband and wife team of physicians, who were diagnosed with cancer. She first asked whether we could give them some kind of Buddhist amulet or talisman to comfort them in their hour of extreme distress and apprehension. We thought of giving each of them one of our *nenju*—strings of beads we hold with our palms pressed together to express our humility and gratitude to the Buddha. But without any familiarity with the Buddhist teachings, they wouldn't find any meaning in the nenju. Instead, we decided to give them a photo reproduction of a statue called Amida Looking Back, along with our thoughts on how one might cope with devastating illness.

This statue of Amida Looking Back, called *Mikaeri no Amida* in Japanese, is found in a temple called Eikando, or Zenrinji, in Kyoto. The wooden statue stands three to four feet high with its head turned to the left, looking back for stragglers. Legend states that back in the thirteenth century, during a religious procession, the monk Eikan was falling behind, so Amida turned back and urged him to hurry up and join the group. For me this figure symbolizes the compassion of Amida, who never abandons anyone and always shows concern, especially for the laggard, the lost, and the confused.

Although we had never met this couple, nor did we know any details about their situation, we wanted to express our deepest feelings and convey some sense of how a Buddhist might deal with a similar difficulty. Our slim hope was that the following reflection might help them through their ordeal.

TO OUR FRIENDS

The Buddha of boundless compassion
  looks back so that no one is left behind,
Beckoning with her left hand,
  "Come as you are!"
And with her right hand held up high, crying,
  "Do not fear for I shall protect you."

When we hear this call, we respond and say
  "NAMU–AMIDA–BUTSU."
Namu *is the lost and confused one,*
  seeking a direction home, and
Amida–butsu *is the Buddha of Immeasurable Light and Life*
  grasping the wayward being, never to abandon.

Immeasurable Light is the light of boundless compassion,
  embracing each Namu-*being in pain and sorrow*
With its warm, comforting rays
  ultimately easing suffering
And opening up deep wisdom—life beyond our control—
  and sharing that sense of reality with all others.

The light of boundless compassion steadily focuses
  on each pain and transforms it
As the jagged ice of immense difficulties melts to become
  the flowing water of true and real life,
Finding its own way slowly
  into the calm ocean, peaceful and serene.

We were overjoyed to hear later from our colleague that the
young couple were doing well—the wife's biopsy for breast can-

cer showed that the growth was benign, and the husband's cancer was treatable, with a good chance of successful recovery. Yet, this was a reminder to us that sooner or later we must all confront "life beyond our control," but we do so within boundless compassion that grasps us never to abandon us.

25

Good and Evil

In the epilogue to the *Tannisho,* Shinran confesses his ignorance concerning good and evil. It is not an ignorance in the ordinary sense but an admission made in the light of boundless compassion that makes us see the constantly shifting parameters of both good and evil. The distinction between the two in common-sensical understanding seems clear-cut, and most of us think that we know what good and evil are, yet the terms abound with confusion, for sooner or later we realize their arbitrary nature. Some may agree with

Hamlet, who said, "There is nothing good or bad but thinking makes it so" (*Hamlet,* Act II, Scene 2). Yet, we cannot pass over the observation by Alexander Solzhenitsyn:

> Gradually it was disclosed to us that the line separating good and evil passes not through states, nor between classes, not between political parties—but right through every human heart and all human hearts.[1]

The shifting connotations of conventional good and bad appear to be no different from terms like "cold" and "hot." In January in Massachusetts, when the temperature sometimes hovers around the zero mark, the weatherman will talk about a "warming trend," meaning that it may go up to five or ten degrees Fahrenheit! Yet, our friend who spends her winters in Puerto Rico tells us that a "cold spell" is forecast there when the temperature goes down to seventy degrees. Once, when we went to Hawaii in January, we went from a temperature of ten degrees in Massachusetts to sixty degrees in this island paradise. It was hot for me even in a T-shirt, but the local people were wearing jackets.

Almost as a daily ritual in the U.S., we see people convicted of murder, sometimes wrongfully, and sentenced to die in the electric chair. Why are the majority of inmates on death row people of color? If murder is wrong and perpetrators should be punished, then why do we decorate soldiers with medals of honor for killing people, even if they are the enemy? In the light of such arbitrary definitions of good and evil, how should we understand these terms from a religious standpoint?

It was Friedrich Nietzsche who undertook a radical analysis of good and evil in his *Genealogy of Morals,* tracing their origins to the *ressentiment*[2] of the lower classes against the elite class. The moral virtues of selflessness, goodness, loving one's neighbor and so forth were once practiced by people of the upper classes as their privilege, but when undertaken by the lower classes they are products of *ressentiment*. This is what Nietzsche calls slave morality, because it is committed with a vengeance that denies their deepest humanity. Thus, he advocated an ethics that arises from an affirmation of self, not from its suppression. Morality should be, above all, liberating and not binding. Whether we agree with his analysis or not, it forces us to reflect on the meaning of good and evil.

Shinran's view on this subject is quoted in the *Tannisho* by his disciple Yuien:

> I do not know what the two, good and evil, really mean. I could say I know what good is, if I knew good as thoroughly and completely as the Tathagata. And I could say I know what evil is, if I knew evil as thoroughly and completely as the Tathagata. But in this impermanent world, like a burning house, all things are empty and vain, therefore, untrue. Only the nembutsu is true, real, and sincere.[3]

Several points are to be noted in this statement. First, the relative nature of good and evil is contrasted to good and evil as seen from the standpoint of the Tathagata or Buddha. That is, the human perspective on good and evil is limited, incomplete, and flawed, negating any absolute notions of good and evil. Second, the statement, "all things are empty and vain," refers to the passing things of the world, but it also rejects our reliance on language as the final arbiter of good and evil. Words are useful but arbitrary, essential in human interaction but possibly misleading. In contrast, the nembutsu is "true, real, and sincere," because it enables us to see our ego-self in operation, its falsity and deceptions in the light of boundless compassion. At the same time, it endows us with humility and gratitude. Third, everything on the horizontal plane of life is critically evaluated from the vertical dimension. From this vantage point we see that the highest ethical good may contain a hidden, self-serving agenda, unknown even to the person involved. Pure good comes from an ethical act arising from living the nembutsu.

The problem of good and evil on the relative plane was confirmed during an incident that occurred during our Buddhist pilgrimage tour to India in the winter of 2000. A group of us visited a school for untouchables in Sujata's Village, located near the River Nairanjana. This was the place where, twenty-five hundred years ago, the emaciated Gautama was offered a bowl of milk from a maiden named Sujata. Having received this life-nourishing drink, he gained the energy to strike off on his own. He then went to Bodhgaya, meditated under the Bo tree, and ultimately attained the supreme enlightenment of Buddhahood.

The purpose of our visit was to give school supplies to the children there. We met about fifteen students, dressed in dark blue uniforms, who were lined up on a bench in the school courtyard. We saw a young Korean monk passing out pencils, notepads, and other items to each of the seated children. Watching this were other village children dressed in rags. After the monk finished, a member of our group also began passing out school supplies, which had been donated by her friends from her home temple. Caught between the privileged students receiving gifts and the village children receiving nothing, she decided to pass out the goods to everyone. Suddenly she was overwhelmed by the children, who began fighting over the supplies. They swarmed around her and other tour members, grabbing whatever they could get their hands on. Not knowing what to do, she began weeping, but, like a pack of wild animals, the children kept after her; and they followed us as we walked back silently to our tour bus.

Was our act of generosity good? How could we have distributed the supplies more fairly? Was there a better way to do so? What does charity really mean? What are the psychic damages done to both the privileged students in school and the village children not in school? We could not leave the money and gifts with the principal, since we were warned that he would simply pocket them for his own use. Countless questions arose as we reflected on our good intentions.

Buddhism differentiates between formal good and genuine good. Our conventional notions of good, normally accepted without question, are called formal good. This good is based upon some universally agreed-upon principle, formed in abstraction, and frequently handed down as an injunction. Genuine good requires us to respond to a given situation, case by case, with full awareness of our limitations and our foremost concern being the needs of the autonomous other. It rejects a predetermined course of action and consequently defies simplistic guidelines. Everything depends on a creative and spontaneous response.

In contrast to Shinran's questioning of good and evil, Paul's confession in Romans 7:19–21 seems to assume a clear knowledge of good and evil, even though admitting culpability: "For I do not do the good I want, but the evil I do not want is what I do. Now if I do what I do not want, it is no longer I that do it, but sin which dwells in me."

Some questions arise from the standpoint of genuine good. What is the basis of Paul's knowledge of good and evil? Is the distinction always clear and unequivocal for him? Are the Ten Commandments or the Sermon on the Mount sufficient as the basis for practicing genuine good? What role does the awareness of sin play in ethical action?

It should be underscored that Shinran's statement does not undermine the distinction between conventional good and evil, but it does question their objective validity. But he also gives us a deeply existential insight into the working of boundless compassion that eradicates the division between self and other, opening up the possibility for com-passion. It leads to ethical action performed with humility and gratefulness, where both the self and other are contained within boundless compassion that is nonjudgmental and all-embracing:

Amida's Primal Vow does not discriminate between the young and old, good and evil—true entrusting alone is essential. The reason is that the Vow is directed to the person burdened with the weight of karmic evil and burning with the flames of blind passion.[4]

This nondiscrimination is to be understood both objectively and personally. That is, absolute compassion does not differentiate between young and old, between good and evil, but at the same time it embraces each of us personally from youth to old age and takes in our total self that inclines to both good and evil.[5] Genuine good can come from only such an awareness, the awareness of boundless compassion that grasps each of us as limited, karma-bound beings.

樹心弘誓佛地

流念難思法海

釋華書

樹心弘誓佛地

流念雜恩法海

PART FOUR

Expanding Horizons

26

Three Grapefruits

A few days before my family and I were leaving Japan in 1968 after a six-year sojourn, my friend from California came to visit and gave us three grapefruits from a carton that he had brought with him. Because of import restrictions, fruits from abroad, such as grapefruits, melons, and grapes, were a rarity and hence ridiculously expensive. A single grapefruit, for example, would cost several thousand yen, equivalent to twenty dollars at the exchange rate at that time.

People bought these exotic, imported fruits primarily to give away as gifts on special occasions.

Since we were returning to California shortly, where grapefruits are in abundance, we decided to give away the three grapefruits. It so happened to be the day that my wife went to her weekly flower-arranging class, so she gave the grapefruits to her teacher. We thought nothing about it, but a couple of days later we received a special-delivery letter from the teacher. Written with brush on traditional Japanese paper and folded carefully, the letter had to be something special. People today use ballpoint pens to dash off missives.

The teacher's letter began with very formal words about the weather, and she expressed appreciation for the three grapefruits. She wrote that she shared the first grapefruit with her grandchildren, who were thrilled with the fragrance and taste of an exotic fruit that they had never seen before. The second grapefruit she peeled and ate together with an old friend whom she hadn't seen for over twenty years, making the reunion a very special event. The third grapefruit she took to a hospital, where her best friend was dying of a terminal illness. She hadn't eaten for more than a week, but when she saw the grapefruit, she wanted to try tasting just a little piece. When she finished the first morsel, she asked for another one, then another one, until she ate half the grapefruit. The family watching all this were in tears, crying and happy that their loved one was enjoying something to eat.

The teacher thanked us profusely from the bottom of her heart for the three grapefruits. My first reaction on reading the letter was, "Thank the grapefruits!" But I also reflected on what Huayen Buddhism says about a small act of giving that has repercussions in an interdependent and interconnected world. According to this tradition, one small act of charity (*dana-paramita*) is said to be equal to countless acts of charity. No one can measure the effects of a single act of giving, for its repercussions are beyond our limited imagination.

The grandchildren will always remember the sweet aroma and taste of their first grapefruit, overlapping with the loving image of their grandmother, even after she is long gone. The two women reminiscing about the past was made all the more memorable with each bite of grapefruit, the good feeling emanating and embracing those around them. The dying friend will live forever in the hearts and minds of her loved ones as she enjoyed each morsel of grapefruit. The letter from the flower-arranging teacher reminds me of the possible relevance of Hua-yen Buddhism for the contemporary world.

In reflecting on *dana-paramita,* however, I am reminded that it requires "three kinds of purity." That is, according to Buddhism, true giving involves the awareness that there is no giver, no gift, and no receiver. Attachments of any kind, whether it be to self as the benefactor, the value of the gift, or the acknowledgment by the receiver nullifies the pure act of giving. In our case we had no attachments, not because we were selfless but simply because we didn't pay for the grapefruits and merely passed them on to the teacher. This might be considered true giving, but it was a fortuitous act and had nothing to do with *dana-paramita* as an act of selfless giving, free of self-interest, which leads to the other shore of enlightenment.

In fact, the true act of *dana-paramita* involves giving up what we cherish the most—ultimately our ego self. I know a Dharma-school teacher who encourages the practice of *dana* in children by setting an example. Once he took his students to give fruits to the homeless. In doing so, he purchased the most expensive fruits at the grocery store. When one mother complained that the homeless did not deserve such extravagance, he explained two important things about true giving. First, it requires some sacrifice on the part of the giver. To give away something that one doesn't need is not *dana.* Second, the act must not be condescending but must show respect to the one who receives the gift. In fact, one is grateful to the recipient who makes the act of giving possible.

Although *dana-paramita* in the true sense is our goal, it is not easy to actually practice it. But, as in the case of our three grapefruits, even if we have to fake it, we want to return something to the world. When such a practice is repeated as often as possible, we may come to realize that just to be alive is a gift, made possible by countless good causes and conditions. In fact, every act of compassion, whether genuine or not, may have a positive significance far beyond our powers of imagination.

27

Forgiveness

In recent years the topic of forgiveness has become a central issue in some circles because of the rising level of anger that is poisoning American society. Research centers are taking a scientific approach to the health benefits of forgiveness as they may affect our well being. It has been shown that anger leads to high blood pressure, but the moment forgiveness takes place the blood pressure immediately drops. Scientific studies also show that anger lowers resistance to infections, and it damages our arteries and even causes heart attacks. I don't doubt the veracity of such studies, and further research is essential, especially today, when we see escalating outbursts of anger in our homes and offices and schools. Road rage and air rage and sideline rage provoke violence and even death.[1]

Forgiveness is considered a major virtue in ethical and religious life, but many questions arise. Is it always a good thing? How does one cope with anger and resentment in order to forgive? What is the relationship between forgiveness and apology? What should one do in the knowledge that some things are impossible to forgive? There is much ambiguity involved in the act of forgiving.

The Buddhist attitude toward forgiveness may shed a different light on the subject. A few years ago, I gave a lecture at a Shin Buddhist temple in Stockton, California, and I briefly described what I had learned about the results of forgiveness research. During the course of discussion, a middle-aged woman who was a member of the temple shared her recent experience at a forgiveness seminar. She said that everyone attending the seminar agreed that we all had to learn to be more forgiving. But she had some reservations about the tone of discussion, for she sensed a tinge of arrogance, a kind of moral superiority, from the participants who gave examples of how they forgave others. When she expressed her doubts concerning some of the examples, she was asked to explain the Buddhist position on forgiveness, so she complied the best she could.

In Buddhist understanding, even before we try to forgive, we have to realize that we are always being forgiven by others. Realistically speaking, whenever we become angry because of what another has done to us, it is close to impossible to be forgiving. In fact, one thinks first of retaliating and taking revenge. Even if one can verbally forgive another, the resentment deep within may continue to smolder, causing irreparable damage. This is the reason that anger is considered a poison in Buddhism, a poison that destroys oneself.

When one admits to the inability to forgive, one may become both more tolerant of one's limitations and more accepting of the other. This open admission might lead to the further realization that one is always being forgiven by other people. When people continue to associate with us and, in some cases, even love us, in spite of our idiosyncrasies, laziness, willfulness, and unpredictable mood changes, we are being forgiven for what we are. This awareness results from appreciating the interdependent and inter-connected nature of reality.

No one can deny that for the majority of us we receive more from our parents than we can give to them. This may also be true in our relationships with our teachers, friends, colleagues, and even strangers who are kind to us. As we deepen our awareness of such a possibility, a sense of appreciation may grow, even for those who create distress and discomfort in our life. This is unthinkable from a commonsense standpoint, but it is an attitude cultivated among Shin Buddhists. A case in point is the following incident that a friend, a graduate student in an Eastern university, once shared with me.

My friend had a roommate, a fellow graduate student in his thirties, who every weekend would go on a drinking binge. He would return to his dorm room drunk at two or three in the morning. He would make a lot of noise—cursing loudly, banging on the walls, kicking the furniture, throwing his books against the wall. Because of this disruptive behavior, my friend could not sleep and would quietly leave the room to find another place to stay for the weekend.

The roommate's behavior grew worse as time passed, and he began circulating rumors about my friend, saying to others such things as "He is strange, he's a Buddhist, he has funny eating habits, he has no friends, he sneaks out in the middle of the night, never returns until morning," and so on. My friend never confronted his roommate about the rumors he was spreading, let alone his drunken behavior every weekend, until at one house meeting the chairperson asked him to share the problem he was having with those present.

So my friend explained to the group the situation that he was having. It was very embarrassing for the roommate, but the chairperson urged him to express his views frankly, admonish his roommate about proper behavior, and try to establish some form of communication. There was tension in the air, filled with the potential for hurt and angry feelings, but my friend never complained about his roommate nor criticized his behavior. Instead, he shared these reflections with the group:

> You know why I never said anything about my roommate? Because I, too, am sometimes like him. I get angry and complain. How can I accuse him of anything? I just realize who I am, I reflect on myself through him. It's none of my business to tell him what to do. If he wants to change, he will. If he doesn't want to change, my saying anything won't make a bit of difference. If he wants to change, or doesn't want to change, either way is fine with me.

And then, turning to his roommate, he continued:

> When I heard that you were bad-mouthing me, I reflected on myself and thought, Yes, yes, that's right, I am just like you, I like to gossip about others, I have strange habits, sometimes I get angry and want to punch someone. Yes, I feel the way you feel about me. We're all the same human beings. Thank you very much for reminding me of who I am and what I can be like.[2]

My friend concluded his remarks by thanking his roommate and said, "People may think that having a roommate like you is a bad experience, but for me it is a good experience, giving me another opportunity to know my true self. For this I am grateful to you."

Forgiveness is a virtue that should be encouraged, but it should be practiced with a sense of humility, arising from the knowledge that one is forgiven even before one thinks of forgiving others. Then, a feeling of gratitude may spontaneously emerge, such that forgiving others or being forgiven is no longer an issue.

28

Caregiver Bodhisattva

Most Americans are familiar with the term *dojo,* since it is associated with the Asian martial arts. This Japanese word came from Buddhism, derived from a Sanskrit term, *bodhimanda,* "the seat of enlightenment," referring to the place where the historical Buddha attained final release from all cravings and karmic bondages. In thirteenth-century Japan, when Shin Buddhism first began, the followers of Shinran did not gather in temples but in *dojo,* ordinary homes used for religious purposes. This term is also widely used for training halls for Zen monks and nuns; it is from this usage that the martial arts adopted the usage of *dojo* for their training centers.

The practice of Shin Buddhism does not require a special meditation hall or a cloistered retreat, because everyday life is our *dojo*, the training place for practicing compassion to others, beginning with our family members. Hence, our *dojo* is our home or our workplace; our practice is pursued, whether living alone or with others. Among the most challenging tasks awaiting us in this *dojo* of everyday life is that of the caregiver. Fraught with all kinds of challenges, difficulties, and demands, it is one of the most stressful tasks that await some of us. Anyone who meets the challenge and provides care for the needy is a bodhisattva, whether the person knows anything about Buddhism or not.

Once when the Buddha was residing in a bamboo grove at Rajagriha, he came upon a monk who was severely ill. When the Buddha asked him if anyone was looking after him, he replied in the negative. Surprised, the Buddha said, "What! You don't have anyone taking care of you? When you were in good health, did you ever take care of the sick?" The monk replied, "No, I never did," whereupon the Buddha said, "That's the reason you must now suffer all by yourself. But don't worry, for I shall take care of you."[1]

Thus, the Buddha became a caregiver to this lonely and sickly monk, cleaning his room, washing his soiled clothes, helping him bathe, changing his bedding, and so on. As he fed him, he shared his thoughts on the Buddha Dharma, and in due course of time, the monk awakened to the ultimate goal of Buddhism: practicing compassion in everyday life. The Buddha then went to the lecture hall and spoke to all the monks:

O monks, you are all brothers in the Sangha. The merit of caregiving is immense, so you should take care of each other in times of poor health and illness. To see a sick monk is no different from seeing a Tathagata.[2]

The following is a story of a Buddhist woman who engaged in caretaking as a challenge on her path to liberation and freedom. A retired oncology nurse, Sets was influenced deeply by her mother, a dignified nembutsu practitioner who lived life graciously, always with compassion, gratitude, and humility. Sets took care of her husband, who was diagnosed four years ago with multifactorial dementia. In spite of the immense stress of caring for him, she used what she learned from her Shin Buddhist tradition about coping with an impossible situation. She was also helped by expressing her thoughts in poetry, guided in her endeavor by poets who encourage caregivers of Alzheimer's patients to express their deepest feelings, negative or positive. Poetry here is not a matter of versification, meter, or rhyme but of manifesting honesty and integrity, something alluded to by Meister Eckhart, who once said that a poet is not a special kind of human being, but every human being is a special kind of poet.

According to Buddhism, the challenge of caregiving can be a form of religious discipline leading to real insight into the human condition, born from tolerance for both one's limitations and the other's plight. A world of compassion opens up, simultaneously transcending and affirming the fragile nature of the human body and psyche. The process of expressing complex feelings objectively in poetry becomes a catharsis that enables a person to become more sensitive and aware, ultimately leading to a shared sense of this unrepeatable human life.

Sets learned to write down her thoughts and reflections in journals, and she put some of them into free verse, openly expressing complaints, confusion, pain, and remorse. Her Shin faith, cultivated through years of deep hearing, helped her to see into her karmic reality and to express things about herself as they are.

186

Whether it eased the burden of caregiving or not, she was able to face "Reality," the title of one of her first attempts at poetry:

> *Anger, resentment and frustrations*
> *Explode like an erupting volcano.*
>
> *Knowing that dementia has robbed my husband*
> *Of his keen memory, his thinking capacity,*
> *Does not help.*
>
> *Caring for him day after day,*
> *Love, compassion and understanding*
> *Disappear into thin air.*
>
> *Sitting quietly,*
> *Facing the Buddha altar,*
> *I meditate on my Reality.*
>
> *My human frailties and limitations*
> *Allow Unhindered Light and Eternal Life*
> *To constantly illuminate and affirm my total being.*
>
> *With palms together,*
> *I bow in gratitude. (March 20, 2000)*[3]

Not only is the reality of human limitation and frailty affirmed, but they become conduits for the flooding light of compassion to illuminate both the caregiver and the care receiver. The luminosity is warm and comforting, in spite of the darkness.

But no amount of religious faith can ease the stark reality of having to deal with a person who has lost all his normal capacities. Only a person who has experienced the immense stress of caring can speak of the challenge to one's sanity, as Sets does in describing an incident as if it just happened, in "Night Watch":

I am awakened abruptly from a deep sleep
At 2:30 a.m.
By the sound of a waterfall.

In the dim night light
I discern the silhouette of a man
Standing and urinating on the carpeted floor
Between two chest of drawers.

I jump out of bed shouting,
"What are you doing?
This is the bedroom
Not the bathroom!"

The blank forlorn look on his face
Sends a message of emptiness.
He does not know where he is,
Nor what is happening
To make me so upset.

I guide him into the shower,
Spray the lower half of his body
With warm water,
Towel dry him and
"Harness" him with Depends
Not giving him a choice, this time.

I tuck him into bed and
He promptly falls asleep
Like a newborn babe.

While her husband falls into deep sleep, unaware of what has happened, Sets must clean up the mess, wondering how long this ordeal will last. Many, many questions arise; the answer is a deafening silence.

Meanwhile, I'm on the floor
With a new roll of Chelsea paper towels
Soaking up the urine
From the carpeted floor.
In the silence of the night
I am struck by
A moment of sadness and helplessness.
"Wow!" there is nothing else for me to do
But clean up this mess!

"With repeated practice
You'll get used to it,"
I hear a caregiver say.

The question for me is
Will I? Will I? Ever?
Be able to accept all this
In Suchness. (June 25, 2000)

Sets' description of her husband's mental state is graphic, made possible by something more working in her life. The eyes of wisdom granted her by the Buddha of Immeasurable Light enable her to see reality just as it is. This awakening to reality, or suchness, as Buddhists call it, is not of her own making; it is made possible by boundless compassion that embraces both her husband and herself, neither of whom has any choice. The husband did not choose to become demented; Sets did not choose to be the sole caregiver. Yet both must fulfill their given karmic roles; there is no exit. In another poem she writes with tenderness and affection:

Assumptions and expectations
Of what I can and should do
Must be erased from my mind.
An inner voice reminds me,
"Be more sensitive and understanding."

His trousers, T-shirt and long-sleeved flannel shirt
Are placed side by side on top of the bed.
He turns them around and around,
Examining them closely.

Not knowing the difference
Between front and back,
He wears his T-shirt reversed,
And inside out at times.
When buttoning his flannel shirt
The buttons are not in alignment
With the button holes.

While cooking breakfast,
I look towards the hallway.
He has walked out of the bedroom
Through the hallway to the dining room.

He is standing beside the chair
Wearing the shirts and boxer shorts only,
Thinking he is properly dressed
To sit at the table to eat his meal.

He looks like a little boy.
His innocence is so revealing

It warms my heart.
I smile and tell him
What he has forgotten to wear;
He looks at my face and chuckles
As a glimmer of awareness dawns.

Together, we put on his khaki trousers,
Embraced in the centerless circle
Of Boundless Life. (May 20, 2000)

When Shin Buddhists speak of true entrusting, it is composed of two aspects which are ultimately one: complete entrusting of oneself to one's karmic situation and total entrusting of oneself to limitless and boundless compassion. The two converge in the person of nembutsu to make that person a true, real, and sincere human being.

After four years of dedicated and loving care, Sets' husband passed away. A chapter in her life closed and her caregiving experience concluded with her final poem, "Going Home."

Patrick is gone now,
He has returned home
To his spiritual home of homes,
To the land of the Buddhas,
A place where his life began
Even before he was born.

I reflect with fond, loving memories
Fifty years of marriage
To a man grounded solidly
Like the Rock of Gibraltar.
Sparse words were spoken to express
His deep felt feelings.
He showed his emotions
Through kind, thoughtful and simple ways.

Experiences shared of joy, pain and sorrow,
Our son and the vegetable garden
Brought him his greatest joy.
We faced many deaths in our family together
Of mothers, fathers, brothers, sisters
Of nieces, nephews, and friends.

As a soldier fighting in the 442nd Combat Team
Three years in Europe during the Second World War,
He faced his own mortality
Seeing the life of his buddies being destroyed
By guns, grenades and artillery fire.

The reality of death made him
See the fragility of life,
Appreciating the gift of his unrepeatable life,
He learned to live fully in the present,
Once saying simply,
"I'm always thinking about life,
And I'm really satisfied with the way my life is."
Each day was a new day and the last day.
(February 7, 2001)

With many precious moments etched in her memory, Sets began a new chapter in her life. She now does an abundance of volunteer work for various causes, the most important being Project Dana, which serves the needs of the elderly, frail, lonely, and sickly on the island of Oahu in Hawaii. This is a concrete example of "selfless giving," *dana-paramita,* put into action. Project Dana started in 1989 and today involves seventeen Shin Buddhist temples, as well as three Catholic churches, one Protestant church, and one Vietnamese Buddhist monastery, all in Honolulu. It celebrated its tenth anniversary in 1999, involving more than seven hundred volunteers over the years.

29

The Inconceivable

as Conceivable

The fundamental basis of Buddhism is called Reality-
as-it-is or dharmakaya-as-suchness. Many synonyms
exist for this term—nirvana, eternal bliss, ultimate
peace, true suchness, and so on—but the most common is "emptiness" (*shunyata*), meaning that nothing
in our world of flux and change has a permanent,
abiding essence. *Dharmakaya* consists of two terms:
the "body" (*kaya*) of "reality as-it-is" (*dharma*), devoid of an essence but forming the basis of life. When
dharma in this primary sense, reality-as-it-is, is articu-

lated by words and concepts, we have the secondary meaning of *dharma* as teaching, such as in Buddha Dharma. Body, of course, is not a physical entity but connotes something akin to such common usage as body of knowledge, body of information, and body of opinion.

Now, Reality-as-it-is points to something beyond the world of human constructs, the world created by our subjective use of language. The moment we utter a word, we create a world of human constructs, such as good and bad, big and small, black and white, love and hate, Massachusetts and California, Canada and Mexico, East and West, and so on, including naming objects and confusing the name for the object. Emptiness in one sense is a radical negation of such human constructs, enabling a person to see things, including the self, as they are. Emptiness empties itself, negating all words, including negation itself, so that we can affirm Reality-as-it-is.

Dharmakaya-as-suchness is said to be inconceivable, incomprehensible, inexpressible, ineffable, immeasurable, unattainable, formless, and unconditioned. This means that it is beyond our rational or conceptual grasp. But one of the great wonders of life is that a movement occurs from within this fundamental reality to enter our world of language, so that we can conceive of the inconceivable. What appears in our consciousness is Reality-that-takes-form or dharmakaya-as-compassion, whose concrete manifestation is the Name-that-calls, NAMU-AMIDA-BUTSU. In the words of Shinran,

> The Buddha's nondiscriminating, unobstructed, and nonexclusive guidance of all sentient beings is likened to the all-embracing waters of the great ocean. From this treasure ocean of oneness, form was manifested, taking the name of Bodhisattva Dharmakara, who, through establishing the unhindered Vow as the cause, became Amida Buddha. For this

reason, Amida is the Tathagata of fulfilled body. Amida has been called "Buddha of unhindered light filling the ten quarters."[1]

The story of Dharmakara Bodhisattva is Reality-that-takes-form given to us as a narrative for the sake of human comprehension. Having fulfilled forty-eight vows on behalf of sentient beings, Dharmakara attains supreme enlightenment and becomes Amida Buddha, the "Buddha of unhindered light filling the ten quarters." This story is ultimately the story of reality being realized in each person, made possible by the working of the invisible Other Power.

Thus, Amida Buddha is not an objective entity but comes alive in each person's awakening to the Name-that-calls, NAMU-AMIDA-BUTSU. That is, as limited, imperfect, vulnerable, and finite beings (*namu*), each of us is granted this unrepeatable life, sustained and protected by boundless compassion (*amida-butsu*). Each saying of NAMU-AMIDA-BUTSU is a call from dharmakaya-as-compassion, reminding us of this fundamental truth, as well as our response to the call that gratefully acknowledges this gift of life.

While the path of Sages considers its ultimate goal to be the direct realization of dharmakaya-as-suchness, the followers of the path of Pure Land regard dharmakaya-as-compassion as the goal of religious life. For foolish beings who have no way to become one with dharmakaya-as-suchness, the Name-that-calls is the ultimate reality.

Zen practitioners and even some Pure Land followers consider dharmakaya-as-compassion as an expedient means to realizing the ineffable and inconceivable dharmakaya-as-suchness. But Shinran regards the former not just as a means but the ultimate goal of the Shin path. The Christian theologian John Cobb, a veteran of Buddhist-Christian dialogue, correctly identifies Shinran's emphasis, as follows:

The conceptual and traditional pressure on Pure Land Buddhists to acknowledge the subordination of Amida to the *Dharma-kaya* is greater than the analogous pressure on Christians to subordinate Christ to the Father. But in Shinran himself this pressure is strongly resisted, at least so far as religion is concerned. In our concrete situation, Amida is ultimate. Amida is ultimate reality *for us,* because ultimate reality for us *is* wise and compassionate.[2]

Once the working of Amida's Primal Vow is fully realized in one's life, then the supreme enlightenment that is dharmakaya-as-suchness occurs by its own accord, necessarily and naturally.

30

The Inconceivable
as Lived

In the previous chapter we discussed the basic foundation of Shin Buddhism in philosophical language, but now we turn to ordinary lay folks and see how they integrate dharmakaya-as-compassion into their daily lives. At a two-week summer session on Shin Buddhism held at the Buddhist Study Center near the campus of the University of Hawaii in August 2000, we studied the poetry contained in *Dharma Treasures: Spiritual Insights from Hawaii's Shin Buddhist Pioneers* and selected verses by Shinran found in *The Collected Works of Shinran,* volume I.

After reading, discussing, reflecting, and pondering the rich and diverse expressions of religiosity in these poems, the more than fifty participants, who had no previous experience writing poetry, expressed themselves in free verse of their own creation.[1] An amazing collection of poems appeared, revealing how much the participants had absorbed the teaching over years of deep hearing, a phenomenon that I call sedimentation.

Sedimentation occurs when years of deep hearing of the call of the Primal Vow leads to a sudden displacement of the calculations of a foolish being by a deeper source of life, beyond any conceptual understanding. The nembutsu comes from this deeper source, as shown in a poem by Sets, who was introduced earlier, in chapter 28.

> *The nembutsu*
> *Comes from the world of silence,*
> *Yet, I hear my voice*
> *Saying* NAMU–AMIDA–BUTSU.

The world of silence is the realm of dharmakaya-as-suchness that is inconceivable, formless, wordless, and colorless. From this realm comes forth the dharmakaya-as-compassion as the nembutsu, the Name-that-calls, which impacts one's life, whether vocalized or not. Sets's intoning is not of her choice; it is a spontaneous response to the call from the deep. The call comes from beyond the far end of the unknown territory that Pema Chodron alludes to when she says, "Things like disappointment and anxiety are messengers telling us that we're about to go into unknown territory."[2]

Some people understand all this intellectually, but the call from boundless compassion demands that we respond with our whole being. Alan, a senior business analyst with a health insurance company, is fully aware of this call but chooses not to respond, giving all kinds of excuses. Behind his denial, however, looms a challenging question.

> *Every day a phone call*
> NAMU–AMIDA–BUTSU *is the message;*
> *It must be "wrong number."*
> *It is not for me.*
> *What darkness covers my heart?*

The last line suggests the reason that the connection is not being made, although the calling from the other side is incessant. When, for example, we are notified about the death of a loved one, it is actually a call alerting us to the precariousness of our fragile human life. Yet, how many of us really heed the call and proceed to learn how to appreciate and cherish this unrepeatable life? Most of us choose to ignore the call, saying "wrong number."

The nembutsu works in a variety of ways, one of which is to make us question our conventional life, its direction, and its ultimate goal. A former medical technologist, Edith, makes this point when she awakens to the ship of boundless compassion that carries her:

> *Birth to age fifty*
> *Carried on the ship of* NAMU–AMIDA–BUTSU,
> *Still I paddled my own boat.*
> *Incredibly, a voice asked,*
> *"Where are you headed?"*

The question "For what purpose am I living?" occurs to many of us in the middle of life. We don't have to be reminded of Dante's question in the *Divine Comedy* to ask, "Where am I headed?" As we reflect on our life, we become faintly aware of the ego-self pushing us forward, yet not really know where it's going.

The very fact of our questioning is evidence that the light of compassion is beginning to illuminate our existence.

A different kind of awareness of the shadow self is revealed in Cecilia's poem, showing a self-awareness that constitutes a major part of Buddhist awakening to the life of delusion. A former teacher and published poet, she writes,

> *Mouth as slippery as an octopus,*
> *Eight-sided, lop-sided, one-sided,*
> *Camouflaged in darkness.*
> NAMU–AMIDA–BUTSU.

> *Although my deceitful mouth*
> *Has not spoken,*
> *Self-righteous thoughts*
> *Crowd my mind.*
> *My biased eyes speak loudly.*
> *I hide my head in shame.*
> NAMU–AMIDA–BUTSU.

Only within the warm light of compassion can a person so openly reveal her dark side without fear of condemnation. The nembutsu repeated here expresses a deep sense of humility accompanying this self-knowledge, as well as a profound gratitude for being shown one's true self embraced by boundless compassion.

A similar insight into the self surfaces in the following poem by Mary, the president of the board of directors of a large Buddhist temple. She took care of her bed-ridden sister for many years, until the sister passed away two years ago. A dedicated caregiver, Mary poured her energy into a compassionate giving of time and energy:

> *With righteous fervor I tended to her needs*
> *Day and night, as she lay hostage*
> *To the crippling disease.*

Then she asked for a measure more,
And I balked.
She made me see me for what I am.
NAMU–AMIDA–BUTSU.

To be shown one's true nature is a kind of revelation, made possible by the light of compassion. It enabled Mary to express her true feelings openly without any feelings of guilt. She was simply being her aware self, and with no burden of guilt, yet with a sense of humility, she was able to continue her caregiving with renewed energy.

No matter how painful, when self-knowledge is realized within boundless compassion, it is a discovery that one might want to celebrate. In fact, Saichi the myokonin, when asked what was his pleasure in life, responded, "My pleasure is this world of delusion; because it turns into the seed of delight in the dharma. NAMU–AMIDA–BUTSU."[3] This reminds us of the story about Carl Jung and Hermann Hesse. When Jung heard that young Hesse was tormented by demons, he promised to chase them away through therapy. Hesse declined the offer, declaring, "If my demons are chased away, my angels will take flight."[4]

Without the working of the light of compassion, deep self-awareness is blinded by the ego, which refuses to admit to any real human imperfection or limitation. But in genuine awakening there occurs an awareness to something greater than the ego–self, whatever you may call it. It is a revelation that comes from the most unexpected source. Jane, an occupational therapist, gives us a simple account of such a happening:

Driving out of the tunnel
Showers up ahead!
Ah, but looking in
The rear-view mirror
A rainbow—lucky me!

201

In fact, when we pause and look around us, we see boundless compassion pursuing us. It seeks us out, it touches us, and it embraces us, never to abandon us, even before we are fully aware of what is happening. Such a realization occurred to Joel, a retired medical technologist, who has been on a quest for Amida all his life:

> *Searching so earnestly for enlightenment—*
> *While stopping to rest,*
> *The Light finds me.*
> NAMU-AMIDA-BUTSU

Once a person realizes the working of boundless compassion, he or she knows that nothing in life is to be wasted, abandoned, or forgotten. Everything, whether a person, an event, or an object, may contain inexhaustible meaning and significance. The reason is evident when we read the following poem by Betty, who is a wife, mother, and grandmother, expressing the optimism inherent in Shin Buddhist experience:

> *All kinds of karma,*
> *Bad karma, good karma.*
> *But with the help of transformation*
> *All become good karma.*
> NAMU-AMIDA-BUTSU.

Transformation is possible by the very fact that Buddhism teaches us that we are all already fully enlightened, although we live in complete ignorance of this elemental fact. This paradox is overcome when we awaken to boundless compassion that makes real the Buddha-nature dormant within us.

We also gain a glimpse into the basic assertion made by many Buddhist philosophers that samsara, the world of delusion, is no different from nirvana, and nirvana is no different from samsara.

Herbert, a retired chemist, renders this in his own words, when he states:

> *Consumed with anger,*
> *The world is an ugly place.*
> *Bathed in happiness,*
> *The world is a wonderful place.*
> *But, aha! the same world.*

This "aha!" is the core experience in the awakening of shinjin, true entrusting to reality-as-it-is.

31

N i r v a n a

The Shin Buddhist understanding of nirvana is clearly stated by Shinran in his work, *Notes on "Essentials of Faith Alone,"* written when he was seventy-seven years old. It is a commentary on a small tract called *Essentials of Faith Alone* by Ryukan, one of the leading disciples of Honen, which contains passages in literary Chinese (*Kanji*) that unlettered people could not decipher. Thus, Shinran wrote the *Notes* in vernacular Japanese, explaining parts of the text as well as including additional material, so that ordinary people might more properly appreciate Ryukan's work. A concluding remark to the *Notes* by Shinran makes clear the intended audience:

> That people of the countryside, who do not know the meanings of written characters and who are painfully and hopelessly ignorant, may easily understand, I have repeated the same things over and over. The educated will probably find this writing peculiar and may ridicule it. But paying no heed to such criticisms, I write only that ignorant people may easily grasp the meaning.[1]

The "ignorant people" here are the illiterate peasants of thirteenth-century Japan. They may not have been able to read the difficult passages quoted from the Chinese; yet the fact that Shinran wrote the *Notes* for their spiritual edification suggests an amazing depth of religious comprehension that was encouraged among them at the time. In fact, their lack of learning and sophistication may have led them to appreciate more directly and intuitively the working of boundless compassion.

One of the central topics in the *Notes on "Essentials of Faith Alone"* is the explication of nirvana by Shinran: "The land of bliss is the realm of nirvana, the uncreated."[2] Here the land of bliss, or the Pure Land, is equated with nirvana, and it denotes "the place where one overturns the delusion of ignorance and realizes supreme enlightenment."[3] This dynamic transformation is possible because the place where it occurs is "the uncreated" (*asamskrita*), the open field of limitless creative possibilities. The uncreated is contrasted to our "created" world, filled with countless human constructs that have built the iron cage in which we imprison ourselves. Leading a constricted life, we are not free and hence are unable to undergo transformation of any kind.

The uncreated, formless, and nameless reality pervades our life and the universe. It is given various names, such as dharmakaya-as-suchness, but Shinran also describes it variously as "ex-

tinction of passions, the uncreated, peaceful happiness, eternal
bliss, true reality, dharma-body, dharma-nature, suchness, oneness,
and Buddha-nature." This list concludes with the following pronouncement:

> Buddha-nature is none other than Tathagata. This Tathagata
> pervades the countless worlds: it fills the hearts and minds of
> the ocean of all beings. Thus, plants, trees, and land all attain
> Buddhahood.[4]

Although we are unaware of it, formless and nameless reality
is basic to life. To awaken us to this fact, this inconceivable reality
moves and comes to us in the form of the dharmakaya-as-compassion. Its dynamic activity comes to us as the working of the
Primal Vow, the vow that was fulfilled by realizing the supreme
enlightenment of all beings. In thirteenth-century Japan this opened
the gates of Buddhism to peoples of all classes, whereas previously
institutional Buddhism had been identified only with the imperial
household and the upper classes.

The working of the Primal Vow means that our religious quest
does not really begin with us; rather, the impetus comes from the
movements of the uncreated itself. Thus, when we entrust ourselves to the Primal Vow, as the result of its working, it is none
other than Buddha-nature actualizing itself in each of us. Shinran
continues the above passage and concludes:

> Since it is with this heart and mind of all sentient beings that
> they entrust themselves to the Vow of the *dharmakaya-as-
> compassion,* this shinjin-awakening is none other than
> Buddha-nature.[5]

The drama of human repentance and liberation occurs in the
realm of the uncreated, the boundless "space" (*akasha*) discussed in
chapter 19.

The creative life, in sum, is based on awakening to the contradictions in life and admission of one's limited powers, not to retreat into self-enclosure but to actively becoming engaged in the task before us, no matter the odds. We work to make changes in the world in a practical, realistic way. This is the basic ethical stance taken by Dr. Rieux in Albert Camus' *The Plague*. He finds his life to be absurd in the face of the relentless epidemic wiping out the city of Oran, but for that very reason he seeks to do whatever he can to fight the devastation, saying, "Heroism and sanctity don't interest me. Only in being myself." In sharp contrast stands Father Paneloux and his sermonizing, which is theologically inane.

In sum, nirvana in Mahayana Buddhism is descriptive of dynamic transformation, where delusion is transformed into enlightenment, where "bits of rubble are transformed into gold." Its ground is beyond time and space and, hence, exceeds our conceptual grasp but not our radical experience.

32

Gratitude

The ultimate expression of gratitude, as well as repentance, is the saying of the Name, NAMU-AMIDA-BUTSU, acknowledging the good karmic circumstances that have blossomed into the true and real life of nembutsu.

Gratitude on the conventional level is a response to favors, kindnesses, and good fortune received from others, but gratitude on the religious level is an affirmation of the gift of life itself, whether we are young or old, poor or wealthy, in good health or bad, living all alone or surrounded by loved ones.

When my eighty-one-year-old father was slowly approaching his end, due to dialysis failure, I flew from my home in Massachusetts to visit him in Los Angeles, where he lived. After spending a few days with him, the time for my return home came. I walked into his bedroom to say good by. When he looked up at me, I said, "Pop, *arigato,* thanks for everything." I wanted to say more, but, overcome with emotion, knowing that this might be the last time I would see him alive, words failed. He immediately responded, "No, no, *arigato* is what I want to say. Thank *you* for everything." My father did not have an easy life, he was far from successful in the ordinary sense, and he experienced poor health toward the end, but for me his total being embodies pure gratitude.

Arigato is derived from the Japanese *arigatai,* which the dictionary defines as "that is too much of a good thing," or "that is impossible to have been." It is based on the Buddhist worldview that any happening is the product of countless causes and conditions, known as dependent co-origination (*pratitya-samutpada*), which is beyond our comprehension or imagination. We cannot even fathom all the elements that contribute to making possible each moment, encounter, or event in our life. That which comes to be, then, is almost miraculous, especially in my own case, making my gratitude even more deep and powerful.

This expression of *arigato* was also the final word of D. T. Suzuki, the pioneer exponent of Zen Buddhism, reflecting his early upbringing by his mother, who lived the Shin Buddhist life. Toward the end of his life, he devoted more and more of his writings to Shin Buddhism, and his final scholarly accomplishment was the translation of Shinran's major work into English under the title *The Kyogyoshinsho: The Collection of Passages Expounding the True Teaching, Living, Faith and Realizing of the Pure Land.*[1]

Describing Suzuki's final moments as he lay dying in a Tokyo hospital, his student and friend Kosho Otani of Tokyo Honganji writes:

> In my observation, the more congenial his attitude became towards Shin Buddhism, the more often he uttered "Thank you." This "Thank you," with his own unique tone, derives from Dr. Suzuki's upbringing in a Shin Buddhist atmosphere in Kanazawa. In other words, Shin Buddhism bloomed in the warmth of his feeling, and Zen manifested itself in the sharpness and resoluteness of his mind; as if the former were his mother and the latter his father, these two elements formed Dr. Daisetz Suzuki.[2]

It is no wonder that Suzuki, and not traditional Shin scholars, was the one to make widely known the phenomenon of *myokonin,* those wonderfully unique personalities of nembutsu faith. While historians may justly criticize them for their limitations living under a feudalistic system, no one can deny the depth of their spirituality.[3]

However, there is another dimension in the act of gratitude that must not be overlooked, and that is repentance, the feeling of inadequacy, regrets over both commission and omission, a sense that one can never truly repay the gifts received. Many years ago a friend told me about a designer who worked in a fashionable Hollywood boutique. A bright and attractive girl, she grew up as the only child of loving parents who gave her much love and support. One day she was swept off her feet by a dashing young man, culminating in a storybook romance and marriage. But one day, after a few years of marriage, her husband abruptly asked for a divorce and left her, with no warning, no questions, and no interest in reconciliation. Angry, bitter, and lonely, she contemplated suicide.

She was thrown into the pit of despair, especially after the tragic loss of both her parent soon thereafter. Her friends left her, she had no confidence, her finances were depleted, and she became ill and despondent. In her sorrow she began to ask herself: Why did this happen to me? For what purpose am I living? Why am I here on earth? Merely to suffer and to be miserable? Is there nothing else in life? These questions came bubbling forth day and night; they lasted for weeks and months.

One summer day she decided to visit her childhood friend in central California. After several hours of driving from Los Angeles across the barren Bakersfield hills, she came upon the lush San Joaquin valley. She stopped to get some fresh air and to stretch her legs, when suddenly she saw spread before her eyes a colorful panorama of wild flowers of every shape, size, and color blanketing the scene before her. Under the deep blue sky, they all seemed to be beckoning and welcoming her to rest her tired body and weary soul. Then she suddenly realized that she was just a traveler passing through, a temporary guest of the world. She thought, "I came with nothing and I'll leave with nothing. Yet the world gives me everything I need. All the wealth in the world, even if I had it, would not belong to me; when I take leave of the world I must leave everything behind."

This revelation created such joy that she wanted to jump up and down; she wanted to yell "thank you" to her husband and friends who had abandoned her. She felt a profound gratitude to everyone for the moments of happiness that she enjoyed and to the world that accommodated a sojourner passing through the world. Her only regret, she confessed, was that her heart was too small to contain the overflowing feeling of gratitude she felt toward everyone. One recalls the famous words of Shakespeare in *Hamlet, Prince of Darkness*: "Beggar that I am, I am even poor in thanks; but I thank you: and sure, dear friends, my thanks are too dear a halfpenny" (Act II, Scene 2).

Here we see a humility born from the fact that we cannot really know all the blessings that are showered upon us. In fact, repentance, the confession of one's inability to be grateful, may be at the core of true gratitude. In fact, Saichi, the myokonin, often said something to that effect:

> *To be grateful is all a lie,*
> *The truth is—there is nothing the matter;*
> *And beyond this there is no peace of mind—*
> "NAMU–AMIDA–BUTSU, NAMU–AMIDA–BUTSU,
> NAMU–AMIDA–BUTSU*!*"
> *(With this I peacefully retire).*[4]

But in the saying of nembutsu the ungrateful expresses gratitude in a quiet, unobtrusive way. The feeling of gratitude emanated has a certain kind of aura, a pervasive quality, that draws attention to it. In the words of Shinran:

> *Such persons are like those who, imbued with incense,*
> *Bear its fragrance on their bodies.*
> *They may be called*
> *Those adorned with the fragrance of light.*[5]

"Fragrance of light" is a metaphor for wisdom, an inner quality that appears in the person of nembutsu, in contrast to those who merely follow the formalities of religion. Haru Matsuda contrasts the two types of people:

> *Although looking great,*
> *Paper flowers have no fragrance*
> *But, oh!, the fragrance*
> *Of a single live flower.*[6]

33

Shinran's Wife

Since the thirteenth century, married clergy have been characteristic of Shin Buddhism, and their wives as *bomori* ("protector of the temple") have played a central role in the tradition.[1] Records are unclear as to the number of wives Shinran may have had, but one name, Eshinni, stands out for her place in history for several reasons, as we shall make clear.

Japanese historians at one time doubted the existence of Shinran, because his name never appears in the historical records or official Buddhist accounts of his time. All doubts concerning his life, however, vanished when ten letters written by his wife, Eshinni, were found in 1921 in the archives of one of the head temples of Shin Buddhism, the Nishi Hongwanji in Kyoto.[2] At the time of the writing Eshinni was living in faraway Echigo Province in northern Japan, while Shinran lived in the capital of Kyoto. The letters are addressed to their youngest daughter, Kakushinni, who also lived in Kyoto with her own family and was at Shinran's bedside when he passed away at the age of ninety. The first two letters date from 1256, and the remainder come after Shinran's death in 1263. The final letter was written in 1268, when Eshinni was eighty-seven or eighty-eight years old. The exact reason for the family maintaining separate households is unclear, but scholars generally agree that Eshinni came from a landowning family in Echigo and returned there with their children to oversee her inheritance.

These letters are significant for three reasons. First, they provide a glimpse into the life of a woman in thirteenth-century Japan who was independent and assertive, well educated, and astute in spiritual matters. She oversaw a large household as the head of the family unit, caring for orphans and several grandchildren, concerned about the well being of indentured servants and worried about food during drought and famine. Eshinni represents a class of women different from the Heian court ladies of the eleventh and twelfth centuries, who produced some of the finest narratives, essays, and poetry, including the *Tale of Genji* by Lady Murasaki, the first novel in world literature.

Second, they shed some light on the details of Shinran's life that are not available elsewhere. Although Shinran was prolific, especially in his seventies and eighties, he never mentions anything about the spiritual odyssey of his earlier years. The few facts concerning his life are reliable and especially valuable, because they come from a source that knew him intimately.

Third, Eshinni demonstrates that the life of an aware Buddhist layperson cannot be delimited by the boundaries of formal Pure

Land doctrines. One of them is the misogynistic view that women had to be transformed into men in order to attain enlightenment, as found in the Thirty-fifth Vow of Amida, which reads:

> May I not gain possession of perfect awakening if, once I have attained buddhahood, any woman in the measureless, inconceivable world systems of all the buddhas in the ten regions of the universe, hears my name in this life and single-mindedly, with joy with confidence and gladness resolves to attain awakening, and despises her female body, and still, when her present life comes to an end, she is again reborn as woman.[3]

This view, inherited from ancient India, seems not to have had any negative effect on Eshinni's faith and spiritual maturity. It suggests that such legacies, maintained by a patriarchal system, exist on a plane separate from the practice and life of a religious person.

That Eshinni was her own person is evident in Letter Seven, where she expresses her wish to have a stupa (*sotoba* in Japanese) built for her, as was the custom of her time among established families. But at the same time she is concerned about its cost, since she has had to sell all her clothes during a famine, so that the children could have food on the table. Famines also caused her servants to run away, and she is worried about an epidemic that is spreading. Eshinni takes full resposibility for maintaining a large household all by herself.

In her old age she struggles with health problems, upset that her condition is not improving, but there is no self-pity. In Letter Nine she writes to Kakushinni:

> I am very happy to be able to write this letter to you, because of the possibility of delivery. Since I last wrote, I have been suffering from diarrhea from about the eighth month of last year. It is very annoying that I do not seem to be get-

ting better. But as far as other matters, my head is filled with cobwebs and nothing is clear because of my age. After all, I am eighty-six years old this year.[4]

Although she complains about her condition, she seems to have been of a strong physical constitution. Soon after this letter, she writes: "I have accumulated the years to an unbelievable age, but I never cough or drool. To this day I have never had to have my back and legs massaged. I work like a dog every day, but this year I am becoming forgetful and my memory has waned."[5] The last extant letter to her daughter was written late into the night:

There are many things that I want to write about, but the messenger says he is leaving early tomorrow morning, so I am writing this in the middle of the night when it is very dark. Thinking that you may not be able to decipher it, I shall quit writing. Please send me some needles. You may give them to this messenger. Would you enclose it in your letter to me? Once again I ask that you let me know in detail the recent news about your children. . . . It is so dark that I don't know how the letter has turned out; it must be difficult trying to read it.[6]

Eshinni's letters are valuable in themselves, but we also learn some facts about Shinran that are not available elsewhere. According to Letter Three, Eshinni tells her daughter about Shinran's hundred-day retreat at Rokkakudo in Kyoto while still a Tendai monk, the message he received in a vision on the ninety-fifth day which prompted him to go to Honen's hermitage for another one hundred days, and his total commitment to Honen's nembutsu teaching.[7]

We have no record of what Honen said to Shinran, but his

constant advice to people was to live life in whatever way that is conducive to enhancing nembutsu practice. Honen frequently said, "If you cannot live the nembutsu as a celibate monk, do so by taking a wife. If you cannot live the nembutsu as a householder, do so by becoming a monk." Such advice gave Shinran the courage to abandon monastic life, eventually marry Eshinni, and have seven children with her.

She adds a postscript to this letter, noting that Shinran was a *doso*, a monk of lower rank, at Mt. Hiei before he left the monastery. This is the only information concerning Shinran's twenty-year stay at the Tendai monastery at Mt. Hiei. She adds that she has copied the message that he received in his Rokkakudo vision on a separate piece of paper, but unfortunately it has been lost. Historians have speculated on the contents of that message, and we cannot go into the details here, but we do know that it prompted Shinran to go directly to visit Honen and seek his guidance.

In Letter Five Eshinni tells of the time that Shinran became ill with fever and kept mumbling, "It must be truly so."[8] The reason for this was that he remembered an earlier episode, when he was still struggling with religious questions, in his early forties. The family was moving from Echigo to the Kanto area, when he saw the hardships of peasant life and, feeling compassion for them, Shinran began reading the Triple Pure Land Sutras a thousand times for their sake. Sutra chanting was a common Buddhist practice that was thought to accumulate merits, which could be turned over to others for their welfare.

When Shinran thus began reading the Triple Sutras, he had a sudden awakening that made him mutter, "It must be truly so":

I suddenly realized the grave mistake I was making, for while I truly felt that repayment of the Buddha's blessing is to believe the teaching for oneself and then to teach others to believe, as in the saying, "To believe in the teaching one-self and make others believe, this is the most difficult of all difficulties," yet I attempted to read the sutra as if to complement the saying of nembutsu which should have been sufficient by itself, Thus, I stopped reading the sutra.[9]

The keen observation that Eshinni made about her husband's inner life and conveyed to her daughter after his death could have been made only by a person of deep religious sensitivity herself.

Letter Three also reveals the high regard that Eshinni had for her husband, as revealed in a dream that she recounts to her daughter. The dream takes place at a dedication ceremony for a recently completed hall. An evening festival is taking place with many brightly lit candles burning. In front of the temple is a horizontal piece of wood, like a *torii,* on which are hung images of Buddha. Eshinni describes what she saw:

One did not even have the ordinary face of the Buddha—the center of the light was like the halo of Buddha and the real figure could not be seen. The other image had without doubt the face of Buddha, and I wondered to myself, "What is the name of this Buddha?" Although I don't know who answered, a reply came back, "That one which shows only rays of light is none other than Honen. He is Bodhisattva Mahasthamaprapta (symbolizing wisdom)." So I asked again, "Then, who is the other image?" The answer came, "that is Bodhisattva Avalokiteshvara (symbolizing compassion). He is none other than Zenshin (Shinran's earlier name)."[10]

Eshinni thought that she should keep the dream to herself. She didn't think anyone would believe her, but she told her husband about seeing Honen in her dream, whereupon Shinran acknowledged the significance of the dream. He said that his master Honen was well known, because of his deep wisdom, as being an incarnation of Bodhisattva Mahasthamaprapta. Eshinni then confides to her daughter:

> Although I never told your father about the dream in which
> I saw him as an incarnation of Bodhisattva Avalokiteshvara,
> since that time I never regarded him as an ordinary man and
> continued to serve him. I hope that you too will fully appreciate what I am saying.[11]

Thus, Eshinni regarded her husband as an incarnation of compassion and assured Kakushinni of his exemplary religious life.

We do not have any record of what Shinran thought of his wife, but since Amida Buddha regards each person as his only child, he must have also seen Eshinni as the sole child of Amida. In fact, according to Shinran, each sentient being is the only child of all the countless Tathagatas or Buddhas in the universe. In his *Hymns of the Pure Land,* he writes:

> *The Tathagata of Light that Surpasses the Sun and Moon*
> *Taught me the nembutsu-samadhi.*
> *The Tathagatas of the ten quarters compassionately regard*
> *Each sentient being as their only child.*[12]

Eshinni's religiosity is rooted in the Primal Vow of boundless compassion that is nonjudgmental and all-embracing. There is no gender distinction here:

> *For all people—men and women, of high station or low—*
> *Saying the Name of Amida is such*
> *That whether one is walking, standing, sitting, or reclining*
> *is of no concern.*[13]

While institutional Buddhism has reflected the social discrimination against women in Asian societies, gender equality in Buddhist scriptures has been espoused, based on the philosophy of emptiness (*shunyata*). Since nothing in the world has permanent, abiding characteristics, including those that differentiate men from women, gender distinction is a delusion. This is central to the famous dialogue between Shariputra, the Buddha's senior disciple, and the Goddess, symbolizing enlightenment, in the *Holy Teaching of Vimalakirti*. Shariputra represents the traditional sexist view and confronts the Goddess about the transformation of female into male in order to qualify for supreme enlightenment. Shariputra is taken to task by the Goddess, who performs miraculous transformations to castigate him. The exchange concludes with the declaration, "The Buddha said, 'In all things, there is neither male nor female.' "[14]

Misogynistic views found in Buddhism are inheritances from such prejudices as summed up in the Five Hindrances and Three Obediences. The Five Hindrances excluded women from becoming Brahma, Indra, Mara, world conqueror, and Buddha; and the Three Obediences asserted that women should obey their parents when young, their husbands when married, and their sons in old age. In order to accommodate such prevalent beliefs, Buddhist scriptures proposed that women could attain enlightenment by becoming transformed into men. The Pure Land view of such a strategy is inherited by Shinran, who writes:

> So profound is Amida's great compassion
> That manifesting inconceivable Buddha-wisdom,
> The Buddha established the Vow of transformation into
>   men.
> Thereby vowing to enable women to attain Buddhahood.[15]

As far as Eshinni is concerned, however, gender transformation does not seem to have been an issue. She does not mention it; in fact, toward the end of her life she tells her daughter that she looks forward to seeing her in the Pure Land, because their meeting in this world seems unlikely. In life Eshinni's major concerns were feeding her family, the well-being of servants, preparation for her own death, and the yearning to see once more her daughter and grandchildren living in faraway Kyoto.

34

Critical Classification
of Doctrines

Shin Buddhism is just one path among the multitudes of paths found in the great Buddhist tradition. How did Shinran see this path in relation to the other paths in Buddhism? What did he think was unique about his path in relation to the others? What, if any, might be the appeal of the Shin Buddhist path for contemporary people? To answer these questions, we now turn to what Buddhist scholars call the critical classification of doctrines.[1] This scheme first arose in Chinese Buddhism to give some semblance of order to the bewildering variety of scriptures, practices, and teachings that came from India from the second to the seventh centuries.[1]

All Buddhist paths aim for transcendence of the world of pain and suffering. Like a worm caught in the darkness of a hollow bamboo, we want to get out into the light of day. There are two ways in which a worm might exit the bamboo tube. First is lengthwise, to move upward and bore through the nodes that divide the tube. But the problem is that the moment one succeeds in passing one, there is still another node. An endless series of nodes await the worm who seeks to get out of the hollow lengthwise.

The second approach is a sideways or crosswise move, so that the worm exits the shaft of the bamboo laterally. When it succeeds in doing so, it immediately finds itself in open space, bathing in the sunlight. There are no obstacles awaiting it, and the exit is immediate and effortless. How do the two approaches differ in dealing with actual life situations?

To take just one example, we find a very Buddhistic idea expressed in Pema Chodron's excellent book *When Things Fall Apart: Heart Advice for Difficult Times*:

> In order to feel compassion for other people, we have to feel compassion for ourselves. In particular, to care about people who are fearful, angry, jealous, overpowered by addictions of all kinds, arrogant, proud, miserly, selfish, mean, you name it—to have compassion and to care for these people means not to run from the pain of finding these things in ourselves. . . .[2]

Now, we should all strive to realize such a practice in our daily life. After all, the ultimate practice in Buddhism, regardless of path or teaching, is to be compassionate to others as well as to the self. Meditation, visualization, and mindfulness are all means to that end. Like the worm trying to burrow through node after node to exit from the bamboo tube, each challenge to be compassionate should inspire a person to work harder and with greater determination.

But what if we cannot, no matter how hard we try? The Pure Land path takes another approach. It is to first awaken to the fact that we are the very objects of compassion, for we live by the sacrifices of others, both known and unknown, by those who love us and forgive our shortcomings, by the gifts of nature that provide food on our tables: vegetables, fish, fowl, and other living things give up their lives, so that we can extend our own life. We realize true gratitude when we are awakened to the fact that the foolish being who fails in being compassionate is the very object of boundless compassion. The power of compassion has already created an opening when we look sideways, so that we move out laterally from the darkness of the bamboo hollow into bright sunlight. How, then, can one not respond by living the life of compassion for oneself and others? This is the way of cultivating compassion in the Pure Land path.

Shinran classified all the schools of Buddhism according to these two movements: lengthwise and crosswise. He then found two categories for each movement: *transcendence,* which is swift and immediate, and *departing,* which takes time and effort. Under "lengthwise transcendence" he placed the esoteric schools of Shingon and Tendai, which promise the attainment of enlightenment in this very body. In "departing lengthwise" he included the schools of Indian origin, such as the Hosso or Yogachara school, which require lengthy periods of dedicated practice. In the current American scene we might include the quasimonastic forms of Zen, Tibetan Buddhism, and Vipassana in the lengthwise category, whether they be instantaneous or gradual.

In contrast to these schools, Shinran placed under "crosswise transcendence" the true teaching of Pure Land, or Shin Buddhism. Here liberation into freedom is immediate, since all is given by the working of boundless compassion. Because it is the invisible Other

Power that makes real our liberation and freedom, self-power efforts ultimately are not relevant. The Pure Land paths that are combined with some kind of self-power practices, such as meditation, visualizing Amida, or repeating nembutsu 60,000 times a day come under "departing crosswise."

Because this classification of doctrines by Shinran was created in the medieval period of Japanese history, it requires updating. This is especially true in North America, where a great variety of Buddhist teachings and practices are converging. But our age of religious pluralism also demands that we take into consideration the immense variety of world religions, clarifying those elements shared in common and identifying the qualities that are unique to Shin Buddhism. We must also take into consideration revolutionary changes in the biological sciences, which promise to radically alter the human landscape. And we cannot neglect the great interest in the psychological aspects of Buddhism in the West. What can Shin Buddhism contribute, if anything, to the many concerns in psychology, psychoanalysis, and mental health?[3]

Epilogue

I once read an essay entitled "The Essence of Shin Buddhism," which showed a remarkable degree of understanding and appreciation. The summation was well written and clearly articulated, and it emphasized the following points, which would appeal to any serious seeker. The author had found the Shin path both attractive and rewarding for the following reasons.

- Living the Nembutsu means to live each moment fully and dynamically.

- This means to be grateful to all the countless seen and unseen forces that constitute our interdependent and interconnected world.
- Humility characterizes the person of nembutsu, a humility born from the awareness of karmic limitations illuminated by and enfolded in the light of boundless compassion.
- The sense of humility opens up our hearts and minds to all sentient and insentient existence, enabling us to converse even with a single wildflower or a single wayside rock.
- This is the life of compassion, born from an expansive sense of oneness with all beings but directed especially to those who are lonely, sickly, tired, and abandoned by the world.
- This way of naturalness and spontaneity responds creatively to the ever-shifting parameters of life.
- The person of nembutsu thus lives in unbounded freedom, always protected by Buddhas and bodhisattvas.

The moment I finished reading this essay, a faint uneasiness overcame me, and I was reminded of Chogyam Trungpa's famous phrase, "spiritual materialism." Clarifying that real spiritual practice is to step out of the "bureaucracy of ego," he elaborates:

This means stepping out of ego's constant desire for a higher, more spiritual, more transcendental version of knowledge, religion, virtue, judgment, comfort or whatever it is that the particular ego is seeking. One must step out of spiritual materialism.[1]

The ego is seductive and misleads in subtle ways, unless one can see through the layers of self-delusions that cover us. This point is made by Wendell Berry, who shares his own experience in his poem, "Breaking,"

Did I believe I had a clear mind?
It was like the water of a river
Flowing shallow over the ice. And now
That the rising water has broken
The ice, I see that what I thought
Was the light is part of the dark.[2]

I find two major problems with this summation of Shin Buddhism. First, the term "essence" is used frequently to express some ideal view of a religious path, but it glosses over the chaotic, messy, and harsh realities that await us on the path of spiritual development. This is the reason that the philosopher Nagarjuna, the father of Mahayana Buddhism, rejected such abstract notions as essence, substance, truth, cause and effect, and so on as totally irrelevant, if not misleading, in our quest to break through delusion into liberation and freedom.

Second, as a consequence of contemplating "essence," another human construct, what follows are the ideal qualities of the nembutsu life that sound good on paper but may be impossible to actualize consistently in everyday living. In fact, the Shin Buddhist teaching awakens us to our reality as infinite finitude, that as finite beings we are absolutely incapable of living in such a manner, no matter how sincerely we yearn to do so. A famous Shin teacher of an earlier age once said that people who believe in such idyllic faith will surely end up in the hell of their own making.

In contrast, we find a realistic model of nembutsu life in the person of Shinran himself. He is made to entrust himself totally to an invisible Other Power, because he is shown that his true reality is the very opposite of an enlightened being. But paradoxically this leads to an awakening, eliciting exuberant joy as he celebrates this life. After marshalling abundant scriptural and relevant writings of past masters to justify the life of nembutsu in his major opus, *The*

True Teaching, Practice and Realization of the Pure Land Way, Shinran
concludes,

> How joyous I am, my heart and mind being rooted in the
> Buddha-ground of the universal Vow, and my thoughts and
> feelings flowing within the ocean of dharma that is beyond
> comprehension! I am deeply aware of the Tathagata's im-
> mense compassion, and I sincerely revere the benevolent
> care behind the masters' teaching activity. My joy grows
> ever fuller, my gratitude and indebtedness ever more com-
> pelling.[3]

Shinran's whole being, *regardless of his psychological state,* is
deeply rooted in the Primal Vow that sustains him; and his
thoughts, *deluded or enlightened,* flow into the ocean of reality as-it-
is. Out of this profound sense of gratitude, his work ends with a
deep wish on behalf of all beings: "May those who see and hear
this work be brought—either through the cause of reverently embracing the teaching or through the condition of [others'] doubt
and slander of it—to manifest shinjin within the power of the Vow
and reveal the incomparable fruit of enlightenment in the land of
peace."[4]

Shinran never claimed to have a special message, nor did he
cry out that he came to save the world. His focus was always on
the working of the Buddha of Immeasurable Light and Life, the
luminosity that enabled him to see through the falsities and shams
he himself was subject to as an ordinary human being. In our age
of spiritual masters, gurus, and charlatans, it is refreshing to hear
the voice of Shinran writing at the age of eighty-six,

> *Not really knowing right from wrong,*
> *Not really knowing false from true,*
> *I lack even small love and small compassion,*
> *And yet, for fame and name, enjoy teaching others.*[5]

But for that very reason he saw himself as the supreme candidate for transformation by boundless compassion. Thus, he could claim without being pretentious or pompous,

> *Although I am without shame or remorse*
> *And totally lack truth or sincerity,*
> *The Name of Amida directed to me*
> *Makes virtues abound in the ten directions of the universe.*[6]

In the long and grand history of Buddhism, Shinran gives hope that the most foolish being, lost and confused, can be transformed into its opposite, for the power of boundless compassion can make "bits of rubble turn into gold." According to the famous words of Tsung-hsiao (1151–1214),

> *One grain of elixir transforms iron into gold;*
> *One word of truth transforms evil karma into good.*[7]

Endnotes

PROLOGUE

1. For the English translations for these Pure Land scriptures, see the recommendations in "For Further Study."

PART ONE

Transformation

Chapter One: Rubble into Gold

1. The expression "causal stage" is peculiar to the Buddhist notion that vows are to be made before embarking on a religious path (cause) that lead

to attainment of Buddhahood (effect). This passage is quoted in *The Collected Works of Shinran,* Vol. I (henceforth *CW I*) (Kyoto: Jodo Shinshu Hongwanji-ha, 1997), p. 456. This volume contains the complete works of Shinran in English translation. Volume II contains introductions to individual works contained in Volume I, glossaries, and reading aids.

2. From the Chinese Vinaya. See J. Takakusu and K. Watanabe, eds., *Taisho Shinshu Daizokyo* (Tokyo: Daizo Shuppan, 1924–34), vol. 2, p. 600ab. Henceforth, *Taisho Tripitaka.*

3. Ibid., p. 334ab.

4. Shunryu Suzuki, *Zen Mind, Beginner's Mind* (New York: Weatherhill, 1982), p. 38.

5. See Article X of Shotoku's "Seventeen Article Constitution" in *Sources of Japanese Tradition* (New York: Columbia University Press, 1960), vol. I, pp. 48–51, where *bonbu* is translated as "simply ordinary men." This awareness of *bonbu* is one quality yet to be cultivated in American Buddhism, according to Issho Fujita, one of the many Buddhist teachers who conducted workshops at the conference "Buddhism in America," in Boston in January 1997. See his article in Japanese in *Silkroad in the Mind* (Saga City: Saga Shinbunsha, 1997), pp. 185–87.

6. Hisako Nakamura, *The Hands and Feet of the Heart* (Los Angeles: The Nembutsu Press, 1991).

7. Ibid., pp. 100–5.

8. Ibid., pp. 151–52.

9. Kusunoki Kyo, ed., *Myokonin monodane Kichibei goroku* (Tokyo: Bunichi Shuppan, 1970), pp. 25–26.

10. From *Metta,* a monthly publication of the Buddhist Study Center, Honolulu (October 2000), p. 4.

11. Mitch Albom, *Tuesdays with Morrie* (New York: Doubleday, 1997), p. 174.

12. Jane Bannard Greene and M. D. Herter Norton, trans., *Letters of Rainer Maria Rilke 1910–1926,* (New York: W. W. Norton & Co., 1972), p. 316.

13. Ibid., p. 373, letter dated November 13, 1925.

14. *The True Teaching, Practice, and Realization* (hereafter cited as *True Teaching*) in *CW I*, p. 48.

Chapter Two: Great Practice and Deep Hearing

1. *True Teaching*, p. 13.

2. Ibid., p. 4.

3. T. S. Eliot, *The Complete Poems and Plays 1909–1950* (Harcourt, Brace, Jovanovich, 1968), p. 136.

4. *True Teaching*, p. 45.

5. Taitetsu Unno, *River of Fire, River of Water: An Introduction to the Pure Land Thought of Shin Buddhism* (New York: Doubleday, 1998), p. 64.

Chapter Three: Progressive Stages of Deep Hearing

1. *True Teaching*, p. 112.

2. I wish to thank Dimitri Bahkroushin of the New York Buddhist Temple for the reference to *toska* and this quotation in a private correspondence.

3. Taitetsu Unno, Epilogue to *Tannisho: A Shin Buddhist Classic* (Honolulu: Buddhist Study Center), p. 33.

4. K. Yamamoto, trans., *The Words of St. Rennyo* (Ube City: The Karinbunko, 1968), Hokei was a disciple of Rennyo (1414–99).

5. Alfred Bloom, *Strategies for Modern Living* (Berkeley: Numata Center, 1992), p. 95.

Chapter Four: Beyond the Psychological

1. *True Teaching,* p. 52.

2. *Hymns of the Pure Land* in *CW I,* p. 335.

3. *True Teaching,* p. 71.

4. Aloysius Pieris, *Love Meets Wisdom* (Maryknoll, N.Y.: Orbis Books, 1988), p. 3.

5. From *Bulletin of Monastic Interreligious Dialogue* 59 (Spring 1982), p. 12.

6. Jean-François Revel and Matthieu Ricard, *The Monk and the Philosopher* (New York: Shocken Books, 1998), p. 172.

7. Author's translation of calligraphies displayed in the Kawai Museum in Kyoto, Japan.

8. *True Teaching,* p. 202.

Chapter Five: Religion and Spirituality

1. C. G. Jung, *Psychology and Religion* (New Haven: Yale University Press, 1961), p. 57.

2. Cathy Song, *The Land of Bliss* (Pittsburgh: Pittsburgh University Press, 2001), pp. 29–30.

3. For English translation of *Shoshinge,* see *CW I, True Teaching,* pp. 69–74.

Chapter Six: Primal Vow

1. Carol P. Christ and Judith Plaskow, eds., *Womanspirit Rising: A Feminist Reader in Religion* (San Francisco: HarperSanFrancisco, 1992), pp. 228–29.

2. *The Gary Snyder Reader* (Washington, D.C.: Counterpoint, 1999), p. 235.

3. *True Teaching,* p. 80.

4. For further discussion, see Taitetsu Unno, *River of Fire, River of Water* pp. 24–25.

5. I. B. Horner, *Women Under Primitive Buddhism* (Delhi: Motilal Banarsidass, 1975), pp. 304–9. For her background, filled with tragic losses, see Pali Text Society Translation Series No. 40, *Elders' Verses II Therigatha* (Oxford: Pali Text Society, 1995), p. 24.

6. From *Dharma Experience Through Poetry* (Honolulu: Buddhist Study Center, 2000), p. 19.

7. From Stephen Mitchell, trans., *The Selected Poetry of Rainer Maria Rilke* (New York: Random House, 1982), p. 304.

8. Ibid., p. 69.

9. C. F. MacIntyre, trans., *Rilke: Selected Poems* (Berkeley and Los Angeles: University of California Press, 1956), p. 127.

Chapter Seven: The Absolute Present

1. Quoted in *Newsweek* (December 20, 1999), p. 83.

2. Henry Wadsworth Longfellow, *Hyperion,* Book II, Chapter 6 (Boston and New York: Houghton Mifflin Co., 1869), p. 144.

3. Mu Soeng, trans., *The Diamond Sutra: Transforming the Way We See the World* (Somerville, Mass.: Wisdom Publications, 2000), pp. 62–63 and 126.

4. "Zenki," *The Eastern Buddhist,* new series, vol. V, no. 1 (May 1972), pp. 74–75.

5. *The Complete Poems and Plays,* p. 119.

6. *Tuesdays with Morrie,* p. 65.

7. Ibid., p. 81.

8. Ibid.

9. Morrie Schwartz, *In His Own Words* (New York: Walker and Co., 1996), p. 92.

10. Author's translation. See alternate version in *Jodo Shinshu Service Book* (Honolulu: Honpa Hongwanji Mission of Hawaii, 1986), p. 120.

11. Morrie Schwartz, *Letting Go* (New York: Dell Publishing, 1996), p. 125.

Chapter Eight: Time at Its Ultimate Limit

1. *Notes on Once-calling and Many-calling* in *CW I,* p. 474.

2. See Nishitani Keiji, "The Problem of Time in Shinran," in *The Eastern Buddhist,* new series, vol. XI, no. 1 (May 1978), pp. 27–33.

3. Quoted in D. T. Suzuki, *Myokonin Asahara Saichi shu* (Tokyo: Shunjusha, 1967), p. 143.

4. Quoted in *Dharma Treasures* (Honolulu: Buddhist Study Center Press, 1995), p. 28.

5. *Notes on "Essentials of Faith Alone"* in *CW I,* p. 455.

6. *Lamp for Latter Ages* in *CW I,* p. 523.

Chapter Nine: Shinjin as True Entrusting

1. Dennis Hirota, ed., *Toward a Contemporary Understanding of Shin Buddhism* (Albany: SUNY Press, 2000), pp. 33–72.

2. *True Teaching,* p. 79.

3. Ibid., p. 85.

4. Ibid., p. 94.

5. Ibid.

6. Ibid.

7. Ibid., p. 95.

8. Ibid., p. 107.

Chapter Ten: A Path Less Taken

1. Mark Epstein, *Going to Pieces without Falling Apart* (New York: Broadway Books, 1998), p. xvi.

2. A friend once remarked that this path might be likened to "The Road Not Taken" by Robert Frost. The conclusion of this poem is ambiguous: Frost thinks he has made the right choice but seems to be unsure; he hopes to be proven right "somewhere ages and ages hence." He also speaks of what has "made all the difference" but never clarifies what that is. See *Selected Poems of Robert Frost* (New York: Holt, Rinehart and Winston, 1955), pp. 71–72.

3. e. e. cummings, *Complete Poems 1913–1962* (Harcourt, Brace, Jovanovich, 1968), p. 755.

4. *The Complete Poems and Plays,* p. 145.

5. "Writers on Writing," *New York Times,* Oct. 23, 2000.

6. *To Know As We Are Known: A Spirituality of Education* (San Francisco: HarperSanFrancisco, 1983), p. 65.

7. *Hymns of the Dharma-Ages* in *CW I,* p. 407.

8. *True Teaching,* p. 56.

9. *Notes on "Essentials of Faith Alone,"* p. 453.

10. *Virtue of the Name of Amida* in *CW I*, p. 656.

PART TWO

Unfolding Awareness

Chapter Eleven: A Wasted Life

1. *The Complete Poems and Plays,* p. 50.

Chapter Twelve: Self-Delusion

1. *Taisho Tripitaka,* vol. 2, p. 793ab.

2. Dogen, *Shobogenzo Genjokoan.* Nishiyama Kosen and John Stevens, trans. *Shobogenzo: The Eye and Treasury of the True Law* (Tokyo: Nakayama Shobo, 1975), vol. I, p. 1.

3. *Showa shinshu Honen Shonin zenshu,* ed. Ishii Kyodo (Tokyo: Jodoshumusho, 1955), p. 473.

4. *Gutoku's Notes* in *CW I*, p. 587.

5. Graham Greene, *The Power and the Glory* (New York: Viking Press, 1972), p. 199.

6. *The Collected Poetry of Francis Thompson* (London: Hodder & Stoughton, 1913), p. 52.

7. *Hymns of the Pure Land,* p. 347.

Endnotes

Chapter Thirteen: Subliminal Self

1. *True Teaching*, p. 85.

2. A similar kind of twofold awareness may be found in the Christian mystic Julian of Norwich, who writes: "Our Lord in his mercy reveals our sin and our feebleness to us by the sweet gracious light of his own self, for our sin is so foul and so horrible that he in his courtesy will not reveal it to us except in the light of his mercy." (*Julian of Norwich: Showings.* New York: Paulist Press, 1978, p. 332.)

Chapter Fourteen: Symbolism of Light

1. N. J. Dawood, trans., *The Koran* (London: Penguin Books, 1956), p. 211.

2. Sarvapalli Radhakrishnan and Charles A. Moore, eds., *A Sourcebook in Indian Philosophy* (Princeton: Princeton University Press, 1957), p. 13.

3. S. Radhakrishnan, trans., *The Principal Upanishads* (New York: Harper and Brothers, 1953), p. 256.

4. *The Collected Poems and Plays of Rabindranath Tagore* (New York: Macmillan, 1954), pp. 22–23.

5. Thomas Cleary, trans., *The Secret of the Golden Flower* (San Francisco: HarperSanFrancisco, 1991), p. 19.

6. Jacques Lusseyran, *And There Was Light* (New York: Parabola Books, 1998), p. 312.

7. Peter Russell, "Mysterious Light," in *Ions: Noetic Science Review* (Dec. 1999–Mar. 2000), p. xx.

8. Hiroyuki Itsuki, *Tariki: Embracing Despair, Discovering Peace* (New York: Kodansha, 2001), p. 126.

9. *Hymns of the Pure Land,* pp. 322–23.

10. Ibid., p. 325.

11. Ibid., p. 326.

12. Ibid., p. 327.

13. Luis Gomez, trans. *The Land of Bliss: The Paradise and Buddha of Measureless Light* (Honolulu: University of Hawai'i and Higashi Honganji Shinshu Otani-ha, 1996), p. 177.

14. *Hymns of the Pure Land Masters* in *CW I,* p. 371.

15. Ibid.

16. Ibid., p. 385.

17. *The Land of Bliss,* p. 186.

Chapter Fifteen: Compassion that Nurtures

1. *Hymns of the Pure Land,* p. 356.

2. Quoted in the *Bulletin of Monastic Interreligious Dialogue* 59 (Spring 1998), p. 13.

3. Quoted in *Asahi Shinbun,* July 3, 1999, p. 3.

4. Aloysius Pieris, *Fire and Water* (New York: Orbis Books, 1996). See review by Rubin L. F. Habito in *Buddhist-Christian Studies,* vol. 20 (2000), pp. 311–15.

5. Quoted in Jean Higgins, "The Feminine Image of God in Shusaku Endo" in *God and Temporality* (New York: Paragon House, 1984), p. 111.

6. See *Tannisho: A Shin Buddhist Classic* (Honolulu: Buddhist Study Center Press, 1996), especially section III.

7. "The Feminine Image of God," p. 101.

8. Shusaku Endo, *Silence* (New York: Taplinger Publishing Co., 1980), p. 259.

9. Ibid., p. 264.

10. See Kenzo Tagawa, *Shukyo to wa nanika* (Tokyo: Yamato shobo, 1984) and *Iesu to iu otoko* (Tokyo: San'ichi shobo, 1980).

11. Quoted in *Iraka no nami,* Nishi Hongwanji Kagoshima Betsuin, ed., Komatsu Art Studio, video documentary.

12. Quoted in *Dharma Treasures,* p. 35.

13. The review was published in *Journal of the Pure Land Buddhist Fellowship,* nos. 14 and 15 (Aug.–Nov. 1998), Jim Pym, ed., Oxfordshire, England.

14. Private correspondence, Aug. 23, 1998.

15. *Tannisho,* p. 4. See also the preface to *True Teaching,* p. 4: "Wholly sincere, indeed, are the words of truth that one is grasped, never to be abandoned, the right dharma all-surpassing and wondrous!"

Chapter Sixteen: Living the Buddha Dharma

1. Quoted in Glen Grant, *Hawaii, the Big Island: A Visit to the Realm of Beauty, History and Fire* (Hong Kong: Mutual Publishing, 1988), p. 62.

2. *Dharma Treasures,* p. 18.

3. *Shinshu Shogyo Zensho* (Kyoto: Kokyo Shoin, 1962), vol. I, p. 688.

4. Quoted in Taira Sato, "The Awakening of Faith in the Myokonin Saichi," *The Eastern Buddhist,* new series, vol. XVIII, no. 1 (Spring 1985), p. 86.

5. Ibid., pp. 86–87.

6. *Dharma Treasures,* p. 17.

7. Ibid., p. 19.

8. Ibid., pp. 23–24.

9. Ibid., p. 36.

10. Ibid.

11. Ibid., p. 8. All quoted poems by Haru Matsuda, pp. 5–9.

12. *True Teaching,* p. 203.

Chapter Seventeen: Personal and Social

1. For the unity of the two, see discussion in Paul H. Ray and Sherry Ruth Anderson, *Cultural Creatives* (New York: Harmony Books, 2000).

2. *Notes on "Essentials of Faith Alone,"* p. 453.

3. *Tannisho,* section XVI, pp. 28–29.

4. *Lamp for the Latter Ages,* in *CW I,* p. 553.

5. Ibid., p. 553–54.

6. *Asahi Shinbun,* June 19, 2000, p. 21. For a brief description of Sugihara's selfless deed, see author's *River of Fire, River of Water,* pp. 84–85.

PART THREE

Life as Creative Act

Chapter Eighteen: Creativity in Shin Life

1. Basho, *Narrow Road to the Deep North and Other Travel Sketches,* Nobuyuki Yuasa, trans. (New York: Penguin Books, 1966), p. 33.

2. Rabindranath Tagore, *Creative Unity* (London: Macmillan and Co., 1922), p. 3.

Chapter Nineteen: Space as Metaphor

1. *The Principal Upanishads.* See p. 392 for *antariksha* and p. 392 for *akasa.*

2. Bunno Kato, et al., trans., *Threefold Lotus Sutra* (Tokyo: Kosei Publishing Co., 1975), p. 244.

3. For detailed analysis, see Kino Kazuyoshi, *Hokekyo no Tankyu* (Kyoto: Heirakuji Shoten, 1962), pp. 238–47.

4. From brochure notes in Loreena McKennitt, *The Book of Secrets,* Warner Bros. compact disc 46719.

5. Robert Murphy, *An Overture to Social Anthropology* (Englewood Cliffs, N.J.: Prentice Hall, 1979), p. 27.

6. Paul Tillich, *Courage to Be* (New Haven: Yale University Press, 1952), p. 81.

7. Bruce Altshuler, *Isamu Noguchi* (New York: Abbeyville Press, 1994), p. 105.

Chapter Twenty: The World-Honored One

1. John Ross Carter and Mahinda Palihawadana, trans., *The Dhammapada* (Oxford University Press, 1987), p. 39.

2. Bengt Hagglund, preface to *The Theologia Germanica of Martin Luther* (New York: Paulist Press, 1980), p. xii.

3. See E. A. Burtt, ed., *The Teachings of the Compassionate Buddha* (New York, The New America Library, 1955), p. 49. For a discussion of this passage, see Taitetsu Unno, "The Many Faces of the Buddha" in Terry C. Muck and Rita M. Gross, eds., *Buddhists Talk about Jesus, Christians Talk about the Buddha* (New York: Continuum, 1999), pp. 138–42.

4. *Tannisho*, p. 33.

Chapter Twenty-One: The Ordinary as Extraordinary

1. Quoted in Tetsuo Unno, *Jodoshinshu Buddhism* (South San Francisco: Heian International, 1980), p. 112.

Chapter Twenty-Two: Two Parables

1. See Taitetsu Unno, "Interior Practice in Shin Buddhism" in *The Pacific World,* new series, no. 6 (Fall 1990), pp. 41–49.

2. *Threefold Lotus Sutra*, pp. 110–25.

3. Ibid., p. 115.

Chapter Twenty-Three: Life as Naturalness: Jinen

1. *Showa shinshu Honen-shonin zenshu*, p. 462. See also Harper Havelock Coates and Ryugaku Ishizuka, *Honen: His Life and Teaching* (Kyoto: Chionin, 1925), p. 396.

2. K. R. Norman, trans., *The Elders' Verses II Therigatha* (Oxford: Pali Text Society, 1995), pp. 14–15 (nos. 114–115). See also Susan Murcott, *The First Buddhist Women* (Berkeley: Parallax Press, 1991), pp. 32–34.

3. Burtt, ed., *The Teaching of the Compassionate Buddha,* p. 32.

4. *Lamp for Latter Ages,* in *CW I,* p. 530.

5. Ibid.

6. Ibid.

7. Quoted in *Harper's,* vol. 298, no. 1785 (February 1999), p. 51.

8. Mary Wada-Roath, ed., *Great Compassion* (Berkeley: Creative Arts Company, 1998), p. 81.

9. Jean Smith, ed., *365 Zen: Daily Readings* (New York: HarperCollins, 1999), p. 132.

10. Burton Watson, trans., *The Collected Works of Chuang-Tzu* (New York: Columbia University Press, 1968), pp. 206–7.

11. *Lamp for Latter Ages,* in *CW I,* p. 530.

Chapter Twenty-Four: Life Beyond Our Control

1. *Tariki,* p. 204.

Chapter Twenty-Five: Good and Evil

1. From *The Gulag Archipelago,* quoted in Jeffrey T. Burton, Mary M. Farrell, Florence B. Lord and Richard W. Lord, eds., *Confinement and Ethnicity: An Overview of World War II Japanese American Relocation Sites* (Tucson, Az.: Western Archeological Conservation Center, 1999).

2. This French word is impossible to translate; it is related to the English word "resentment" but with physiological as much as psychological con-

tent, such that it becomes a character trait. It is said to be a "bitter emotion based on a sense of inferiority and frustrated vindictiveness. It is a thoroughly *reactive* emotion, provoked by the successes of others." See Robert C. Solomon and Kathleen M. Higgins, *What Nietzsche Really Said* (New York: Schocken Books, 2000), p. 114.

3. *Tannisho,* p. 34.

4. Ibid., p. 4.

5. See Jitsuen Kakehashi, "Good and Evil Embraced by Boundless Compassion," in *Dharma Rain* (New York: New York Buddhist Church, 2001), pp. 3–10.

PART FOUR

Expanding Horizons

Chapter Twenty-Seven: Forgiveness

1. The *New York Times* (May 6, 2001, p. 1) ran a story titled "New Rules for Soccer Parents: 1) No Yelling, 2) No Hitting Ref."

2. Private correspondence, October 15, 1999.

Chapter Twenty-Eight: Caregiver Bodhisattva

1. *Taisho Tripitaka,* vol. 2, pp. 766b–767a.

2. Ibid.

3. All poems by Sets are from personal correspondence, later contained in *Mosaic Moon,* ed. Frances H. Kakugawa (Honolulu: Watermark Publishers, 2002).

Endnotes

Chapter Twenty-Nine: The Inconceivable as Conceivable

1. *Notes on Once-calling and Many-Calling,* in *CW I,* p. 486.

2. John Cobb, *Beyond Dialogue: Toward a Mutual Transformation of Christianity and Buddhism* (Philadelphia: Fortress Press, 1982), pp. 125–26.

Chapter Thirty: The Inconceivable as Lived

1. All poems quoted below are from the booklet *Dharma Experience Through Poetry.*

2. Pema Chodron, *When Things Fall Apart* (Boston: Shambhala Publications, 1997), p. 14.

3. D. T. Suzuki, *Mysticism: Christian and Buddhist* (New York: Harper and Brothers, 1957), p. 191.

4. This story may be apocryphal, but it reflects Hesse's thought on creativity. See his letter to Jung of September 1934, in *Soul of the Age: Selected Letters of Herman Hesse 1891–1962* (New York: Farrar, Straus and Giroux, 1991), pp. 186–87.

Chapter Thirty-One: Nirvana

1. *Notes on "Essentials of Faith Alone,"* p. 469.

2. Ibid., p. 460.

3. Ibid.

4. Ibid., p. 461.

5. Ibid.

Endnotes

Chapter Thirty-Two: Gratitude

1. Published in Kyoto by Shinshu Otaniha (1973).

2. Quoted in *The Eastern Buddhist,* new series, vol. II, no. 1 (August 1967), pp. 164–65.

3. For some of Suzuki's critical views on the myokonin, see Bando Shojun, "D. T. Suzuki and Pure Land Buddhism," in *The Eastern Buddhist,* new series, vol. XIV, no. 2 (Autumn 1981), pp. 132–36.

4. Quoted in D. T. Suzuki, *Mysticism: Christian and Buddhist,* p. 211.

5. *Hymns of the Pure Land,* in *CW I,* p. 357.

6. *Dharma Treasures,* p. 9.

Chapter Thirty-Three: Shinran's Wife

1. See Jane Imamura, *Kaikyo: Opening the Dharma, Memoirs of a Buddhist Priest's Wife in America* (Honolulu: Buddhist Study Center Press, 1998).

2. James Dobbins, "Women's Birth in Pure Land as Women: Intimations from the Letters of Eshinni," in *The Eastern Buddhist,* new series, vol. XXVIII, no. 1, pp. 108–22.

3. *The Land of Bliss,* p. 170.

4. Yoshiko Otani, *Eshinni: Wife of Shinran Shonin* (Kyoto: Jodo Shinshu Hongwanji-ha, 1990), p. 99.

5. Ibid., p. 101.

6. Ibid., pp. 103–4.

7. Ibid., pp. 91–94.

8. Ibid., p. 95.

9. Ibid., pp. 95–96.

10. Ibid., p. 92.

11. Ibid., p. 93.

12. *Hymns of the Pure Land,* p. 356.

13. *Hymns of the Pure Land Masters,* in *CW I,* p. 385.

14. Robert Thurman, trans., *Holy Teaching of Vimalakirti,* (University Park: Pennsylvania State University Press, 1976), p. 62.

15. *Hymns of the Pure Land,* p. 341.

Chapter Thirty-Four: Critical Classification of Doctrines

1. For Shinran's own classification, see *True Teaching,* p. 114 and *Gutoku's Notes,* in *CW I,* pp. 587–88.

2. *When Things Fall Apart,* p. 93.

3. Helpful guidelines in considering this issue can be found in the article "East Meets West: Dialogues and Departures" by Victoria Jean Dimidjian and Fred Eppsteiner in *Readings: A Journal of Reviews and Commentary in Mental Health,* vol. 15, no. 1 (March 2000), pp. 12–17.

Epilogue

1. Chogyam Trungpa, *Cutting Through Spiritual Materialism* (Berkeley: Shambhala, 1973), p. 15.

2. Wendell Berry, *The Collected Poems, 1957–1982* (San Francisco: North Point Press, 1984), p. 146.

3. *True Teaching*, p. 291.

4. Ibid.

5. *Hymns of the Dharma-Ages*, p. 429.

6. Ibid., p. 421.

7. *True Teaching*, p. 64.

Glossary

Ākāsha Sanskrit word for "space," meaning the realm of spirituality, or true and real life, in contradistinction to the ordinary sense of space as a human construct.

Amida Contraction of *amitābha* (Immeasurable Light) and *amitāyus* (Immeasurable Life) into Amida in East Asian Buddhism.

Amida Buddha One of innumerable Buddhas in Mahayana Buddhism, its distinctive quality being boundless compassion that is nonjudgmental and all-embracing. Sometimes rendered as the Buddha of Immeasurable Light and Immeasurable Life.

Avalokiteshvara Bodhisattva of compassion, called *Kuan-yin* in Chinese and *Kannon* in Japanese. In the crown of this bodhisattva sits the figure of Amida Buddha.

Avataṃsaka Sūtra One of the principal Mahayana scriptures quoted frequently by Shinran in his major works.

Birth in the Pure Land Symbolic expression for the transcendence of delusion. While such a birth was thought to come after death in traditional Pure Land thought, Shinran spoke of its realization here and now; for example, he states, "Although my defiled body remains in samsara, my mind and heart plays in the Pure Land."

Blind passion (klesha) Passions that arise from the darkness of ignorance (*avidyā*), such as greed, anger, and folly.

Bodhisattva A seeker on the path of enlightenment, as well as an idealized expression of enlightenment, for example, the manifestations of compassion (Kannon, Avalokiteshvara) and wisdom (Seishi, Mahāsthāmaprāpta).

Bonbu (pṛthagjana) A foolish being of deep self-centeredness who is unaware of the working of boundless compassion that sustains all life.

Buddha Awakened or Enlightened One. Originally denoted only the historical Buddha, Shakyamuni, but later, in Mahayana Buddhism, countless Buddhas inhabit their respective universes.

Ch'i (ki in Japanese) Vital life force emanating from the centrum, the pit of the abdomen.

Darkness of ignorance (*avidyā*) Source of human suffering, both personal and collective.

Deep Hearing (*monpō*) Central practice in Shin Buddhism, which is not simply auditory but involves the transformation of the whole person in responding to the call of boundless compassion.

Defilements A synonym for blind passions.

Dharmākara Bodhisattva Paradigmatic figure that identifies with the suffering of sentient beings and fulfills vows to resolve all suffering, ultimately achieving Buddhahood.

Dharmakāya-as-compassion Manifestation of true reality (dharmakāya-as-suchness), which appears in the human world in its most accessible form as the nembutsu, or the Name-that-calls, NAMU-AMIDA-BUTSU.

Dharmakāya-as-suchness True reality that is inconceivable, inexpressible, unfathomable, and formless, necessitating its appearance in our world as NAMU-AMIDA-BUTSU.

Dōjō From the Sanskrit *bodhi-manda,* or seat of enlightenment. Any training hall for religious practice. In Shin Buddhism our home and workplace is our *dojo.*

Eighteenth Vow Also called the Primal Vow of Amida proclaimed in the Larger Sutra which insures the liberation and freedom of the most foolish and ignorant.

Exclusion Clause A warning contained in the Eighteenth Vow of Amida against committing the five transgressions and slandering the Dharma. But paradoxically, it also underscores those who are the primary object of the Primal Vow. The five transgressions are causing harm to father, mother, monk, and Buddha and creating disharmony in the Sangha.

Evil Doer (akunin) A term that sums up human finitude, foibles, and shortcomings, expressed in a variety of ways in Japanese that defy easy translation into English. Examples are such adjectives as *asamashii* (ungrateful, shallow-minded), *nasakenai* (wretched, painfully imperfect), *oroka* (foolish, ignorant, mistake-prone), *tsumaranai* (worthless, useless), *guchi oi* (complainer, grumbler), *minikui* (unsightly, shameful), *tsumi bukai* (steeped in karmic hindrance), and so on.

Evil karma Karma connotes individual responsibility; that is, one's state in life is one's own doing and no one else is responsible for it. Since human action, motivated by self-concern, frequently causes suffering to oneself and others, it is described as "evil," a term covering a wide spectrum of motivation and behavior.

Foolish being, see *bonbu.*

Gassho Literally, "palms placed together," signifying the giving up of the ego-self to the other, whether Amida Buddha or other people.

Great Practice The activity or "practice" of the Buddha becomes manifest in a person as the saying of nembutsu. The focus is not on individual religious practice but on the "great" boundless compassion working on behalf of all beings.

Jinen The power of each being (*ji*) realizing its full potential, becoming what it was meant to become (*nen*).

Kalpa Inconceivable eons of time.

Karmic evil Synonymous with evil karma.

Ki-hō ittai The union (*ittai*) of dharmic reality (*hō*) and each human potential (*ki*), insuring the liberation and freedom of karma-bound beings.

Licensed evil (*zōaku-muge*) A heresy based on a distortion of the absolute compassion of Amida Buddha as condoning evil acts, based on the argument that nothing can obstruct the working of the Primal Vow. In fact, the true appreciation of this compassion leads a person to become humble and inspires one to become a better person.

Lotus Sutra The most popular Mahayana Buddhist scripture in East Asia, an abbreviation for *Saddharma-puṇḍarīka Sūtra* or *The Sutra of the Lotus Flower of the Wonderful Law.*

Mādhyamika A major philosophical school of Indian Buddhism, founded by Nāgārjuna, who lived in the second and third centuries C.E.

Mahāsthāmaprāpta Bodhisattva of wisdom who, together with the bodhisattva of compassion (Kannon, Avalokiteshvara), manifests the two aspects of Amida Buddha.

Myōkōnin Literally, "wonderful, good person." Devout, sincere followers of Shin Buddhism, generally from the lower classes in premodern times, with very little formal education.

Name (*myōgō*) Self-articulation of inconceivable reality, dharmakaya-as-suchness, reaching human beings in the form of dharmakaya-as-compassion, whose concrete manifestation is the Name.

Name-that-calls Interpretive translation for *nembutsu*, NAMU-AMIDA-BUTSU, which is the beckoning call to human beings from the side of Amida Buddha to take leave of delusion and awaken to reality-as-it-is.

NAMU-AMIDA-BUTSU The unity of relative beings (*namu*) given life within boundless compassion (*amida-butsu* or Amida Buddha). But this division is conceptual and is to be completely overcome in death, whereby each *namu* becomes *amida-butsu*.

Nembutsu Saying of the Name, *NAMU-AMIDA-BUTSU*, known as recitative nembutsu, in contrast to meditative nembutsu, a method of contemplation. Also used synonymously with *myōgō,* or the Name.

Nirvāna Sūtra The final sermon of the historical Buddha, known as the *Mahāparinirvāna-sūtra.*

Other Power (*tariki*) The boundless compassion of Amida Buddha, which underlies all dualistic notions of self and other. According to Shinran, "Other Power means to be free of any form of calculations (*hakarai*)" (*CW I*, p. 537).

Oya Literally, "parent," but used in a deeply personal and intimate way to refer to Amida, enhanced by adding the honorific, *sama,* which connotes familiarity.

Path of Sages All schools other than Pure Land Buddhism; also used generically to refer to those who affirm self-power on the religious path.

Path of Pure Land In contrast to the path of Sages, which is primarily monastic, in Japanese Buddhism the path of Pure Land has been primarily a lay movement.

Practice Forms of self-discipline aimed at training a person mentally, psychologically, and somatically from a deluded state to an enlightened state.

Primal Vow (*pūrva-pranidhāna*) The radical wish of life itself for each sentient being to attain liberation and freedom. The basic condition fulfilled by Bodhisattva Dharmakara to become Amida Buddha.

Pure Land Translation from the Chinese *ching-t'u* (*jōdo* in Japanese). The term as such is not found in Sanskrit, the closest being the phrase "purification of the Buddha Land." Shinran describes it as the Land of Immeasurable Light, referring not to a place that emanates light but a realization whenever one is illuminated by the light of compassion.

Samādhi Deep absorption or concentrated meditation.

Saṃkhāra Subconscious tendency resulting from countless past lives.

Saṃsāra The repeated life of delusion, translated as the ocean of birth-and-death.

Self-cultivation (*gyō, shugyō*) Mental and somatic training, involving effort, patience, and dedication to a path—religious, ethical, or artistic.

Self-power Reliance on human effort alone to break through delusion into enlightenment.

Shinjin True entrusting realized as the result of being infused by the light of boundless compassion, enabling a person to affirm karmic limitations and thereby become transformed.

Shōshinge A summation of Shin Buddhism, including the purport of the three Pure Land Sutras and the seven masters of the Shin lineage composed by Shinran. It concludes the chapter on practice in his major opus, *The True Teaching, Practice and Realization of the Pure Land Way,* found in *CW I,* pp. 69–74. This work is used for daily chanting in temples and before home altars in traditional Shin Buddhist families.

Tathāgata A synonym of the Buddha widely used in Mahayana Buddhism. The term has two connotations: *tathā-gata,* or One who has gone to suchness, and *tathā-āgata,* or One who has come from the world of suchness. The latter, *nyorai* in Japanese, is widely used in East Asia.

Tendai A major Buddhist school, founded by Saicho (767–822) with its headquarters atop Mt. Hiei, northeast of Kyoto.

Three Minds The three basic elements in Shin spirituality—sincere mind, joyful trust, and aspiration for the Pure Land—all qualities arising from Amida Buddha or Other Power and not from any self-generated effort.

Transformation The working of boundless compassion which transmutes evil into its opposite without nullifying it.

Wisdom (prajñā) In the path of Sages one strives to achieve wisdom through self-discipline, practice, and effort, whereas in the path of Pure Land one is endowed with wisdom by the Buddha.

Yogāchāra One of two major Buddhist philosophical systems that originated in India in the fourth century C.E. Known as the Hossō school in Japan.

For Further Study

The following are recommended English translations of the three basic scriptures of Shin Buddhism: the *Larger Sukhavati-vyuha Sutra* and the *Smaller Sukhavati-vyuha Sutra* in *The Land of Bliss: The Paradise of the Buddha of Measureless Light,* translated by Luis Gomez (Honolulu: University of Hawaii Press and Higashi Honganji Shinshu Otani-ha, 1996); and the *Sutra on the Contemplation of the Buddha of Immeasurable Life* (1984), published by the Ryukoku University Translation Center, headed by Meiji Yamada. These sutras are cited in our text in their abbreviated forms: *Larger Sutra, Smaller Sutra,* and *Contemplation Sutra.*

Complete English translations of these three sutras are contained in a single volume, entitled *The Three Pure Land Sutras,* translated by Hisao Inagaki and published by Bukkyo Dendo Kyokai (BDK) (Berkeley: Numata Center for Buddhist Research and Publication, 1995). This is now available on *www.ne. jp/asahi/pureland-buddhism/amida-net/dharmakara-index. htm.*

In order to gain a proper understanding of Shinran's religious and philosophical thought, the reader should turn to *The Collected Works of Shinran* (cited in the endnotes as *CW*) in two volumes, published by the Jodo-shinshu Hongwanji-ha, Kyoto, Japan (1997). Volume I contains all the works by Shinran in English translation, a project sponsored by the Hongwanji International Center in Kyoto, which took twenty years to complete by a group of scholars lead by Yoshifumi Ueda and the head translator, Dennis Hirota. Volume II includes excellent introductions to each text found in Volume I, a glossary of Shin Buddhist terms, and other study aids.

Volume I opens with the translation of Shinran's major opus, popularly known in Japanese as *Kyo gyo shin sho,* although the full title in the original is *Ken Jodo shinjitsu kyo gyo sho monrui,* translated in *CW* as *The True Teaching, Practice and Realization of the Pure Land Way.* Since this work is written in the formal style of Buddhist scholarship in thirteenth-century Japan, marshaling innumerable quotations from scripture and commentaries, it defies easy reading. Thus, the beginner is advised to first read Shinran's shorter works, especially his notes or commentaries and extant letters and his poetic works, also in Volume I. This work was also translated into English by D. T. Suzuki under the title *The Kyogyoshinsho: The Collection of Passages Expounding the True Teaching, Living, Faith and Realizing of the Pure Land* (Kyoto: Shinshu Otaniha, 1973). It contains the first four of the six chapters.

While there are countless introductory works on Shinran's thought and Shin Buddhism in the Japanese language, very little has been translated into English. Among them, the most readable is *Tariki: Embracing Despair, Discovering Joy* (Kodansha, 1999) by

Hiroyuki Itsuki, a leading novelist in Japan. An introduction to Shin Buddhism, written from a contemporary American perspective, is my experimental venture, *River of Fire, River of Water: An Introduction to the Pure Land Thought of Shin Buddhism.* Also recommended is Hee Sing Keel's *Understanding Shinran* (Fremont, Cal.: Asian Humanities Press, 1995). Written by a Christian theologian, it is both sympathetic and critical of Shinran's thought, and it should be read together with Alfred Bloom's review article responding to Keel's criticisms in the journal, *Buddhist-Christian Studies,* vol. 20 (2000), pp. 95–113.

We do not have a book-length biography of Shinran yet, but those interested should find *The Life of Shinran Shonin: The Journey of Self Acceptance* (1994) by Alfred Bloom helpful. Originally published in the journal *Numen,* it was revised and issued by the Institute of Buddhist Studies in Berkeley, California.

An important work that discusses the words of Shinran, as well as controversies surrounding them a short time after his death, is the *Tannisho* (Lamenting the Deviations). Compiled by a disciple by the name of Yuien, it gives a good insight into Shinran's religious thought. Two books are recommended for appreciating this text: the author's *Tannisho: A Shin Buddhist Classic* (Honolulu: Buddhist Study Center Press, 2nd ed., 1996) and Alfred Bloom's *Strategies for Modern Living: A Commentary with the Text of the Tannisho* (Berkeley: Numata Center for Buddhist Translation and Research, 1992).

Shinran's contributions owe much to the life and thought of Honen, whose legacy is contained in his major work, *Honen's Senchakushu: Passages on the Selection of the Nembutsu in the Original Vow,* translated by the *Senchakshu* English Translation Project (University of Hawai'i and Sogo Bukkyo Kenkyujo of Taisho University, 1998). An interesting reading of Honen is found in a book by Soho Machida, a former Zen monk, in his *Renegade Monk: Honen and Japanese Pure Land Buddhism* (Berkeley: University of California Press, 1999).

For Shinran's legacy leading to the formation of Jodo Shinshu or Shin Buddhism as the largest denomination in Japanese Buddhism, the reader may turn to several works. *Rennyo: The Second Founder of Shin Buddhism* by Minor L. Rogers and Ann T. Rogers (Berkeley: Asian Humanities Press, 1991); *Bearer of Light: The Life and Thought of Rennyo* by Jitsuen Kakehashi (Los Angeles: Pure Land Publications, 1999); and *Jodo Shinshu: Shin Buddhism in Medieval Japan* by James C. Dobbins (Bloomington: Indiana University Press, 1989). The thoughts of a charismatic Shin priest in the twentieth century are found in *Shout of Buddha: Writings of Haya Akegarasu,* translated by Gyoko Saito and Joan Seany (Chicago: The Orchid Press, 1977).

Shin Buddhism is represented in the U.S., by the Buddhist Churches of America (with sixty temples) and the Honpa Hongwanji Mission of Hawaii (with thirty temples). The best work on the subject is *Ocean: An Introduction to Jodo Shinshu Buddhism in America* by Kenneth K. Tanaka (Berkeley: Wisdom-Ocean Publications, 1997). Also recommended is Jane Imamura's work, *Kaikyo—Opening the Dharma: Memoirs of a Buddhist Priest's Wife in America* (Honolulu: Buddhist Study Center Press, 1998). There are about ten active Shin Buddhist centers in Europe, and one of the leaders is Jim Pym of England, whose work, *You Don't Have to Sit on the Floor: Bringing the Insights and Tools of Buddhism into Everyday Life* (London: Rider, 2001) is also recommended.

An important work for the future development of Shin Buddhism in the West is the volume edited by Dennis Hirota, entitled *Toward a Contemporary Understanding of Pure Land Buddhism: Creating a Shin Buddhist Theology in a Religiously Plural World* (Albany: State University of New York Press, 2000).

All of the above books should be available at The Buddhist Bookstore, 1727 Octavia St., San Francisco, CA 94109; (415) 776–7877.

Index

Abhidharma Buddhism, 150
After Life (film), 86–87
Amida (Amita) Buddha, 2, 3, 4, 5, 12,
  15, 21, 66, 68, 77, 194–95, 253–54;
  Amitabha or Amitayus
  (Immeasurable Light or Life), 2, 105;
  bonbu and, 15–16; compassion that
  nurtures, 107–13; Forty-eight Vows,
  3, 70, 95, 215; light and, 101, 103;
  Looking Back (*Mikaeri no Amida*),
  162; *Oya-sama* (Japanese), 107–8,
  116; salvific activity, 24–25; "six syl-
  lable name," 116–17; sincere mind,
  69; as Tathagata, 24–25; twelve
  names, 103. *See also* NAMU-AMIDA-
  BUTSU
Amstutz, Galen, 123
And There Was Light (Lusseyran), 102
Anger, 119, 179–83
Atman, 100, 139
Avatamsaka Sutra, 144, 254
Awakening, 12; deep hearing and, 28,
  35–36; Dharmakara Bodhisattva, 50,
  194–95; nembutsu and, 12–13, 17,
  117–18; time and, 63–66; social
  ethics and, 142

265

Basho, 133–34
Berry, Wendell, 228
Bhaishajyaguru, 2
Birth of Tragedy, The (Nietzsche), 133
Blind passion, 95, 102, 104, 132, 254
Bloom, Alfred, 33, 68
Bodhisattva, 3, 29, 39, 139, 185, 254
Bonbu (foolish beings), 15–17, 21–22, 24, 31, 35, 69, 80, 94, 119, 195, 254
Borges, Jorge Luis, 157–58
Brihadaranyaka-Upanishad, 100–1
Buddha: Dharma, 19, 33, 35, 68, 90, 91, 103, 114–22, 139, 156–57, 185–86, 194; -nature, 205–6; various, 2, 107
"Buddha in the Glory, The" (Rilke), 53
Buddhism: basic tenets, 11, 49, 185–86, 223–24; body-mind unity, 40–42; branches, 2; classification of doctrines, 222–25; goal of practice, 75, 185, 223; good, 169; history, 1–2, 4, 25; Japanese, 15, 25; misogyny in, 215, 219–21; Reality as-it-is (*dharma*) and, 193–96; "realize" used in, 26–27; self-knowledge and, 90; Western interest, 40, 74–75, 225
Burnt Norton (Eliot), 59

Camby, Marcus, 86
Camus, Albert, 206
Caregiving, 185–92, 200–1
Chandogya Upanishad, 139
Chanting, 44–46, 217
Charity (*dana-paramita*), 176–78, 192
Ch'i (ki), 58, 101, 254
Chodron, Pema, 198, 223
Christianity, 99, 108–11, 195–96
Chuang-tzu, 158
Cobb, John, 195–96
Collected Works of Shinran, The, 198, 266
Compassion (*karuna*), 3, 5–6, 32, 185–92, 223, 224; acts of, 177–78, 184–92; boundless (*amida-butsu*), 12, 15, 20, 21, 25, 28, 29, 35, 37, 38, 51–52, 68, 76, 91–92, 118, 119–22, 125–26, 146, 152–53, 221, 224;

karma and 30–31, 39, 51; parable, 13–14; praising, 38; self-, 223; *sesshu-fusha* (grasped, never to be abandoned), 25, 93, 162–63, 170; transformation and, 21, 24
Confucius, 33
Contemplation Sutra, 3–4, 69–70
Creativity, 131, 133–36, 206–7
Crow Dog, Mary, 221
Culapanthaka, 13
cummings, e. e., 76

Dalai Lama, 55–56
Darkness of ignorance (*avidya*), 255
Death, 20–21, 58, 60; awakening and, 60, 85; deathbed ritual, 66; funeral rite, Shin, 61; parable, 51; Pure Land and, 66; transformation and, 18–19, 20
Deep hearing (*monpo*), 19, 25, 26–29, 198; beyond the psychological, 37–42; five stages, 27–28, 30–36; of nembutsu, 24, 28, 35, 52; twofold purpose, 31; ultimate goal, Shinjin, 68; total involvement and, 40–42
Deep mind, 69–70
Defilements (*klesha*), 13, 255
Departing, 224
Dependent co-origination, 209
Dharma, 147, 193–96
Dharmakaya, 64, 193; -as-compassion, 194–96, 197–203, 206, 255; -as-suchness, 193, 198, 255
Dharmata (thingness), 91
Dharma Treasures (Muneto, ed.), 115–16, 197–98
Diamond Sutra, 57
Divine Comedy (Dante), 199
Dogen, 58, 90
Dojo, 28, 184–185, 255
Dry Salvages, The (Eliot), 26
Duino Elegies (Rilke), 21

Easy Path, 76, 78, 91, 258
Eckhart, Meister, 186
Ego-self, 5, 31, 35, 42, 75–76, 79, 131, 132, 144–46, 155, 167, 177, 199, 201, 228–29; *toska* and, 32

Index

Eliot, T. S., 26, 59, 77, 88
Emptiness (*shunyata*), 3, 39, 193, 219
Endo, Shusaku, 109–10
Enlightenment, 11, 22, 36, 39, 50, 158, 195–96, 205; "aspiration to be born in the Pure Land," 28–29, 39, 65, 69, 70, 71; Primal Vow and, 78–79
Epstein, Mark, 75
Eshinni, wife of Shinran, 213–19
"Essence of Shin Buddhism (essay)," 227–29
Evil doer (*akunin*), 256
Existenz, 144

"Fetters" (Song), 45–46
Fire and Water (Pieris), 109
Five Gates of Contemplation, 38–40
Flower Garland Sutra, 144
Foot, George, 111–13
Forgiveness, 179–83
Four Noble Truths, 14, 31, 132, 160–61
Fromm, Erich, 109

Genealogy of Morals (Nietzsche), 166–67
Genshin, 38, 47
"Going Home" (Sets), 191–92
Good and evil, 165–70
Gratitude (*arigato*), 127, 167, 208–12, 224; life of, 28, 35–36
Great practice, 24–25, 256

Hagglund, Bengt, 145–46
Hamlet (Shakespeare), 166, 211
Hawaii, 114–15, 118, 120–22, 192
"Hear" (ideograph), 52
Hesse, Hermann, 201
Hirota, Dennis, 68
Hokei, 33
Holy Teaching of Vimalakirti, 220
Honen of Japan, 4–5, 25, 47, 91, 154, 155, 157, 204, 216–17
"Hound of Heaven, The" (Thompson), 92
Humility, 5, 127, 167, 211
Hymns of the Pure Land (Shinran), 104–5, 219

Ichigo-ichiye, 58
Ichitaro, 148, 158
Ikenaga, Archbishop Leo, 108
Inouye, Father Yoji, 108–9
Interpreting Amida (Amstutz), 123–24
Isaiah *60:19*, 99
Itsuki, Hiroyuki, 103, 161

Jinen, 154–59, 256
Jinen-honi (Shinran), 157, 159
John: *8:12*, 99; *12:35–36*, 99
Judaism, 99
Jung, Carl, 44, 201

Kalpa, 117, 256; "Koti of," 22, 32
Karma: collective, 140; evil and, 21, 95, 104, 116, 123, 125, 157, 256; foolish being and, 21–22; "good karmic past" (*shukuen*), 153; liberation from, 28, 30–31, 32–33, 35, 39, 51; self and, 5–6; suffering and, 12, 14, 21, 32, 75–76
Kata, 41
Kawai, Kanjiro, 41
Ki-ho ittai, 94–97, 257
Kichibei, 18–19
Koran, 99–100
Kuan-yin (Kannon), 52, 148, 254, 257
Kuohsi, Paul Shan, 40
Kyogyoshinsho, The (Suzuki), 209

Larger Sutra, 3, 30, 31, 37, 48, 69
Lennon, John, 86
Letting Go (Schwartz), 62
Licensed evil (*zoaku-muge*), 125, 257
Life (*amitayus*), 5, 81; change and, 57, 220; creativity in, 131–36, 206–7; death and, 19, 51, 61; dignity of all things, 147–49; as *dojo*, 28; interconnectedness, 38; lack of control over, 162; light and, 105–6; as naturalness (*jinen*), 154–59; nembutsu and, 24, 27, 35; questioning the meaning, 85–88, 199–200, 211; suffering, 12, 14, 31, 32, 131; task of, 142; tragedy of a wasted, 86–88; ups and downs, 34–35; value, 11, 19, 20, 61–62
Light, 98–106
Little Gidding (Eliot), 77

Index

Longfellow, Henry Wadsworth, 56–57
Lotus Sutra, 139, 151–52, 257
Luke *15:11–32*, 151
Lusseyran, Jacques, 102

Madhyamika Buddhism, 257
Mahasthamaprapta, 257
Mahayana Buddhism, 2, 21, 161, 207, 229, 254; Buddhas in, 107
Makinodan, Mitsuyo, 65
Malunkyaputta, 156
Marty, Martin, 44
Matsuda, Haru, 120–21, 212
McKennitt, Loreena, 140
Meditation, 75
Monk and the Philosopher (Revel and Ricard), 40
Mosu, 25
Mourning, Alonzo, 86
Murphy, Frank, 115
Murphy, Robert, 140
Myokonin, 257

Nagarjuna, 47, 78, 229, 257
Nakamura, Hisako, 17–18
Nakamura, Iwaichi, 116, 117–18
Name (*myogo*), 257, 258; -that-calls (*nembutsu*), 257
NAMU-AMIDA-BUTSU (*nembutsu*), 5, 6, 12–13, 17, 21–22, 23–24, 27, 31, 33, 35, 37, 38, 52–53, 64, 71–72, 81, 112, 113, 119–22, 126, 134, 135–36, 157, 167, 194, 198–99, 200, 208–12, 255, 257, 258
Nenju, 162
Nietzsche, Friedrich, 87–88, 133, 166
"Night Watch" (Sets), 188–89
Nirvana, 202, 204–7; reality-as-such-ness, 193, 198, 255; Sutra, 258
Nishida, Kitaro, 133
Nishi Hongwanji temple, Kyoto, 214
Noguchi, Isamu, 141
Noh theater, 41, 139
No-self (*anatta, anatman*), 75
Notes on "Essentials of Faith Alone" (Shinran), 204–5

Ondobo, ondogyo (fellow seekers), 76
Onizuka, Ellison, 121–22

"On White Ashes" (Rennyo), 61
Oshima, Jutaro, 111, 119
Oshima, Tai, 119
Otani, Kosho, 210
Other Power, 37, 76, 79–80, 117, 124, 157, 161, 195, 224–25, 229, 258
Overture to Social Anthropology, An (Murphy), 140

Palmer, Parker, 78
Patacara, 155
Path of Sages, 74–75, 78, 79, 80, 91, 119, 195, 258
Pieris, Aloysius, 40, 109
Plague, The (Camus), 207
Poetry and poets, 186
Power and the Glory, The (Greene), 92
Practice, 258
Primal Vow (Eighteenth Vow, *purva pranidhana*), 3, 24, 30, 31, 32–33, 48–54, 64–66, 68, 76, 157, 170, 196, 198, 221, 206, 230, 255, 258; enlightenment and, 78–90, 80; exclusion clause, 50–51, 255–56; three basic attitudes, 69–71; universal emancipation, 50–51
Project Dana, 192
Psalms *27:1*, 99
Pure Land (*sukhavati*), 64, 65–66, 77, 122, 161, 259; aspiration for birth in, 28–29, 39, 65, 69, 70, 71; death and, 66; as nirvana, 205; path of, 74, 75–80, 258. *See also* Shin Buddhism

"Reality" (Sets), 187
Reality as-it-is (*dharma*), 193–96, 203
Religion, 44–46; choosing a path, 73–74, 222–23; faith-oriented, 79; *shu-kyo*, 78
Rennyo, 61
Repentance, 126, 127, 210–12
Revel, Jean-François, 40
Ricard, Matthieu, 40
Rilke, Rainer Maria, 20–21, 53
River of Fire, River of Water (Unno), 111–12
Rodrigues, Sebastian, 110

Romans: *5:20*, 92; *7:19–21*, 169
Russell, Peter, 102–3
Ryukan, 204

Saichi, 64–65, 116, 201, 212
Samadhi, 95, 259; of Constant Practice, 4
Samkhara, 259
Samsara, 17, 29, 34–35, 145, 202, 259; transcending, 28, 74, 91, 223–24
Sasaki, Chiyono, 118–19
Sasaki, Joshu, 41
Sato, Fumio, 126
Sato, Taira, 116–17
Sawaki, Kodo, 158
Schwartz, Morrie, 20, 59–60, 62
Secret of the Golden Flower, 101
Sedimentation, 19–20, 198
Self-cultivation (*shugyo*), 41–42, 259
Self-delusion, 89–93, 101–2, 144–45
Self-knowledge: attaining, 27, 33, 90, 182–83, 201; as *bonbu*, 21–22; *ki-ho ittai* and, 94–97, 257; *manas*, 95–96
Self-power, 27, 79, 225
Sets (poet), 186–92, 198
Shakyamuni Buddha (historical), 2, 13, 185, 254; *bodhimanda* of, 184; Culapanthaka and, 13; ego-self and, 75–76; Four Noble Truths, 14, 31, 132; infant, 142, 143; parables, 13–14, 51, 156; remains, 138; self-knowledge, 90; World-Honored One, 142, 143, 144
Shan-tao of China, 47, 116
Shantih (peace), 88
Shariputra, 220
Shin Buddhism (Jodo-shinshu), 2–3, 4–5, 227–31; Amerian, 124; basic tenet of Honen, 4–5; birth in Pure Land, 28–29, 254; "bits of rubble into gold," 11–22, 145, 207, 230; contemporary appeal, 222–25; creative nature, 131, 133–36; depth analysis of human consciousness, 150; descriptive nature, 131, 132, 134; emptiness in, 39; evocative nature, 132–33; goal of religious life, 195–96; "great practice," 24; in

Hawaii, 115, 118, 120–22; in Japan, 4, 115, 161; *ki-ho ittai*, 94–97, 257; married clergy, 213–14, 217; *myokonin*, 115, 116, 210; *nembutsu, see* NAMU-AMIDA-BUTSU (*nembutsu*); "one thought-moment," 63–64; opening school to the masses, 25, 75, 206; paths, 74, 75–80, 91, 224–25; persecution, 111; practice, 184–85; practice of compassion, 5–6, 12, 224–25, *see also* Primal Vow; primary goal, 68; scriptures, 4; self-cultivation in, 150–53; seven masters, 47; social ethics and political action, 123–27; Triple Sutras, 3, 217–18
Shingon practice, 4, 138, 224
Shinjin, 63–64, 66, 67–72, 94, 116, 203, 259; faith vs., 67, 68, 79
Shinran, 5, 21, 24, 25, 32–33, 38, 45, 63–66, 68, 69–71, 78–79, 80, 81, 91, 93, 94, 104–5, 106, 108, 124, 125, 146, 157, 159, 165, 167, 169, 194–96, 198, 204–5, 206, 212, 217, 229–31, 254; wife's letters, 213-19
Shoshinge, 45, 47, 259
Shotoku, Prince, 15
Silence (Endo), 109–10
Sincere mind, 69, 70
Single Mind, 69
Smaller Sutra, 3
Snyder, Gary, 49
Social ethics, 123–27
Solzhenitsyn, Alexander, 166
Song, Cathy, 45
Space (*akasha*), 136, 137–42, 206, 253
Spirituality, 43–44
"Spiritual materialism," 228
Straight Way, 74
Stupa, 136, 137–38, 139, 141, 215
Suffering, 12, 14, 21, 32, 131, 156–57, 255; bodhisattva of compassion (Kuanyin) and, 52; existential (*toska*), 32
Sugiharo, Chiune, 126
Surya, 100
Suzuki, D. T., 209–10
Suzuki, Shunryu, 14

Tagore, Rabindranath, 101, 136
Tale of Genji (Lady Murasaki), 4, 214
T'an-luan, 47, 79, 122
Tannisho, 109, 146, 165, 167
Tao, 101
Tao-ch'o, 47, 74
Tariki (Itsuki), 103, 161
Tathagata, 24–25, 68, 71, 167, 206, 259
Tathata (suchness), 25, 91
Tattva (thatness), 91
Tea ceremony, 58–59
Tendai practice, 4, 138, 224, 260
Te-shan Hsuan-chien, 57
Theologia Germanica, 145–46
Theravada Buddhism, 2
Three Minds, 69–70, 260
Tibetan Buddhism, 2, 74, 75, 138, 224
Tillich, Paul, 141
Time, 56–57; Dalai Lama on, 55–56; here and now, 19, 20, 55–60, 77; Japanese New Year, 56; tea ceremony and, 58–59; ultimate limit, 63–66
Tohei, Akira, 134–35
"To Our Friends" (poem), 163
Transcendence, 28, 74, 91; lengthwise vs. crosswise, 223–25
Transformation ("bits of rubble into gold"), 11–22, 202, 205, 207, 230, 260; in death, 18–19; deep hearing and, 27, 35–36, 41–42; foolish beings awakening, 15–17, 21–22, 31; illumination of darkness, 25, 35–36; in life, 17–18, 27, 31, 131–36; nembutsu and, 23–24, 35; personal, 124–25; women into men, 220–21
Triple Pure Land Sutras, 3, 217–18
True Teaching, Practice and Realization of the Pure Land Way (Shinran), 229–30
Trungpa, Chogyam, 228
Tsung-hsiao, 231

Tuesdays with Morrie (Albom), 20, 59–60
Tz'u-min, 12

Uncreated (asamskrita) 205-6
"Unhindered light," 25
Unno, Taitetsu, 15, 16–17, 111–12; aikido lessons, 134–35; choice of Pure Land path, 75–80; dream, 148–49; father's death, 209; grapefruit analogy, 175–76; millennium and, 55–56; personal aspiration, 28; pilgrimage 2000, 168–69; Stockton, CA, lecture, 180; subconscious and, 96; sutra chanting, 44–45

Vairochana Buddha, 2, 138
Vasubandhu of India, 38, 47
Vipassana Buddhism, 2, 74, 75, 224
Virtues, 25

Walker, Alice, 77
Waste Land, The (Eliot), 88
When Things Fall Apart (Chodron), 223
White Nights (Dostoevsky), 32
"Who the Buddhas Are (Snyder)," 49
Wisdom (prajna), 13, 27, 35, 71–72, 80–81, 117, 260; "fragrance of light," 212
Womanspirit Rising (Christ and Plaskow), 49
World-Honored One, 142, 143, 144, 146
Worship, 38

Yin-yang, 98
Yogachara Buddhism, 95, 150, 224, 260

Zen Buddhism, 2, 14, 74, 75, 134, 195, 209, 224
Zen Mind, Beginner's Mind (Suzuki), 14
Zoroastrianism, 98

CPSIA information can be obtained
at www.ICGtesting.com
Printed in the USA
FSOW02n2030141217
42463FS